D1383520

The
Education *of*
the Presidents
of the United States

VOLUME 1: GEORGE WASHINGTON TO JAMES BUCHANAN

CAREY's
FRANKLIN ALMANACK,
FOR THE YEAR 1823,
BEING THE SEVENTH AFTER LEAP YEAR.
CONTAINING:
The rising, setting, places, and eclipses of the Sun and Moon; the
southing, phases, age, and latitude of the Moon; longitude of her
ascending Node, &c. the geocentric places and aspects of the
Planets; the rising, setting, and southing of the most conspicuous
Planets and fixed Stars; the passage of Alioth over the Meridian;
the equation of time, Sun's declination, and time of high water at
Philadelphia, &c. Also, the increase, decrease, and length of
Days, with the festivals, &c.

TAYLOR.

The
Education *of*
the Presidents
of the United States

VOLUME 1: GEORGE WASHINGTON TO JAMES BUCHANAN

General Editor
Fred L. Israel
Department of History
City College of New York

Associate Editors
Michael Kelly
Department of History
The Gilman School

Hal Marcovitz
Staff Reporter
Morning Call (Allentown, PA)

Introduction by Arthur M. Schlesinger, jr.
Albert Schweitzer Chair in the Humanities
City University of New York

MASON CREST PUBLISHERS
PHILADELPHIA

Mason Crest Publishers
370 Reed Road
Broomall, PA 19008
www.masoncrest.com

1 3 5 7 9 8 6 4 2
First Printing

Library of Congress Cataloging-in-Publication Data

The education of the presidents of the United States / Fred L. Israel,
general editor ; introduction by Arthur M. Schlesinger, Jr.
    p. cm.
Includes bibliographical references (p.) and index.
  ISBN 1-59084-546-3 (Set) — ISBN 1-59084-547-1 (v. 1)—ISBN
1-59084-548-X (v. 2)—ISBN 1-59084-549-8 (v. 3)
  1. Presidents—United States—Biography.
  2. Presidents—Education—United States. [1. Presidents—Education.]
  I. Israel, Fred L.
  E176.1E34 2004
  973'.09'9—dc22
                         2003023310

Table of Contents

VOLUME 1: GEORGE WASHINGTON TO JAMES BUCHANAN

Introduction

I t is singular that in the United States, a country fascinated both by education and by presidents, no one has written a book on the education of American presidents until this one. One reason may be that the link between American presidents and their education is complex and problematic.

Presidents, like everyone else, are shaped by the totality of their experiences of life. Anything may be a means to education for those who possess what T. S. Eliot called an "experiencing nature." "A whale-ship," observes Ishmael in *Moby Dick*, "was my Yale College and my Harvard." The greatest American autobiography deals very little with formal schooling but is entitled *The Education of Henry Adams*.

So experience shapes presidents. But there is a narrower definition of education as something taught in schools and colleges—as in answers to the question, "Where were you educated?" Formal instruction is tangible and measurable. History, however, reveals no necessary relationship between the quality of the schooling presidents had undergone as students and the quality of their performance in the White House.

Thus by common consent our three greatest presidents were George Washington, Abraham Lincoln, and Franklin D. Roosevelt. Washington and Lincoln had very little formal schooling. FDR had the best formal schooling the country could supply—Groton, Harvard, Columbia Law School. But, whatever their education, they were all great presidents.

Nor was it true that in Washington's and Lincoln's day college education was rare. After all, Washington's successors were John Adams, Harvard 1755; Thomas Jefferson, William and Mary 1762; James Madison, College of New Jersey (now Princeton) 1771; James Monroe, William and Mary 1776; and John Quincy Adams, Harvard 1787. Not until our seventh chief executive—Andrew Jackson—did the United States have another president who had not gone to college.

A total of nine presidents never attended college at all. Besides Washington, Jackson, and Lincoln, the educationally challenged in the nineteenth century were Martin Van Buren, Zachary Taylor, Millard Fillmore, Andrew Johnson, and Grover Cleveland. Even in the twentieth century, that century of higher education for the masses, we had one president who never made it to college. This was Harry S. Truman. Yet historians and political scientists customarily place Truman in the "near great" category.

On the other hand, the three most conspicuous "failed" presidents—James Buchanan, Dickinson 1809; Herbert Hoover, Stanford 1895; Richard M. Nixon, Whittier 1934—were all college men. An AB degree is thus no guarantee of success in the White House, nor is its absence a guarantee of failure.

But Washington, Lincoln, and Truman keenly lamented the inadequacy of their schooling. Washington and Lincoln hit upon the same adjective to describe their education—"defective." Washington believed that the radical American experiment in democracy required popular education to make it work. In his farewell address he called on his fellow citizens to promote "institutions for the general diffusion of knowledge. In proportion as the structure of a government gives force to public opinion, it is essential that public opinion should be enlightened."

President Washington had a specific institution in mind. "That a National University in *this* country is a thing to be desired, has always been my decided opinion," he wrote his vice president, John Adams, in 1795, "and the appropriation of ground and funds in the Federal City, have long been contemplated." The same year he told Jefferson of his dream of a university in the nation's capital where students would become "better acquainted with the principles of law, and government" and could learn from an international faculty "among whom some of the most celebrated characters in Scotland, in this line, I am told may be obtained." By recruiting students from all across the land, Washington added, a national university would "contribute to wear off those prejudices, and unreasonable jealousies, which prevent or weaken friendships and impair the harmony of the Union."

He took the case to Congress the next year in his eighth and last annual message. "The common education of a portion of our Youth from every quarter, well deserves attention.... A primary object of such a National Institution should be, the education of our Youth in the science of *Government*." Congress, Washington said, had no more pressing duty "than to patronize a plan for communicating it to those, who are to be the future guardians of the liberties of the Country."

The father of his country found very little support for his educational program. With renewed urgency he returned to the subject in the will drafted six months before his death in 1799. Here Washington expressed once again his "ardent wish" for a national university and left a substantial bequest toward its endowment. None of Washington's successors, however, has echoed his call for a national university.

Lincoln as an aspiring young politician called education "the most important subject which we as a people can be engaged in," and as president in 1862 he signed the Morrill Land Grant Act, providing public funds for state universities and colleges. Thus two great presidents, denied much formal education themselves, strove to improve educational facilities and amenities for the future guardians of American liberties.

The story of forty-two men (no women so far, alas) with diverse educational preparations for the presidency is compelling in its variety and its drama. And a word should be said about the vivid and imaginative illustrations that accompany and enhance the text.

The conclusion of this work? Surely it is that there are many roads to the White House.

—Arthur M. Schlesinger, jr.

Foreword

In the Declaration of Independence of 1776, Thomas Jefferson listed more than thirty grievances against the king of England. Eleven years later, in writing the Constitution of the United States, the Founding Fathers quite naturally rejected a hereditary monarch or powerful head of state. Instead, they established an elected chief executive with a specific term of office. Article II, Section 1 of the Constitution explains, "The executive Power shall be vested in a President of the United States of America. He shall hold Office during the Term of four Years." There are formal constitutional requirements: one must be a "natural born citizen," at least thirty-five years old, and a resident of the United States for fourteen years. The constitution refers to the president as "he." It was probably beyond the thought process of the Founding Fathers that a woman, or a man who was not white, would ever be considered. The Twenty-second Amendment (1951), which deals with term limitations, uses "person" in referring to the president, recognizing that a woman could serve in that office.

The United States was the first nation to have an elected president—and a president with a stated term of office. Every four years since the adoption of the Constitution in 1789, the nation has held a presidential election. Elections have been held even during major economic disruptions and war.

The forty-two white men who have served as president seem to have very little else in common.[1] Five were never elected. John Tyler, Millard Fillmore, Andrew Johnson, Chester Arthur, and Gerald Ford entered office through death, assassination, or resignation of their predecessor. Each failed to remain in office, either through personal choice or political fate.

Some of these forty-two men were surprisingly strong-willed, while others were simply miscast. Although Abraham Lincoln prevented the permanent break-up of the Union and Woodrow Wilson and Franklin D. Roosevelt each confronted a world war, most presidents were average men doing the best they could in a complicated job. Likewise, there does not seem to be a pattern in the kind of person whom the voters have chosen to be their leader. They have been as young as John F. Kennedy (forty-three) and as old as Ronald Reagan (sixty-nine), intellectuals like Madison, Taft, and Wilson or plain thinkers like the great Jackson and the failed Harding. Personality types have run the gamut, from the ebullient spirits of the two Roosevelts and Truman to the taciturn Coolidge and dour Nixon. The Adamses, John and John Quincy, were father and son, as are George H. W. Bush and George

---

[1]George W. Bush is the forty-third president of the United States. However, forty-two men have served in that office as Grover Cleveland is considered the twenty-second and twenty-fourth president because of his non-consecutive terms.

W. Bush. Benjamin Harrison's grandfather was William Henry Harrison of "Old Tippecanoe" fame. Theodore Roosevelt was Franklin's admired cousin. They have come from states across the country, from Vermont to California. Mostly they have come to the White House from Congress and from governors' mansions. Six generals have been elected to the presidency. And, except for the tragic Civil War that followed the 1860 election of Lincoln, the electorate has always accepted the peaceful transfer of power.

Many of these men sought the responsibilities of the presidency. Others landed there by accident. Regardless, each man occupied a position of power and did his best to exercise leadership as he understood it. Each had the opportunity to make major decisions both in foreign and domestic matters that affected the direction of the nation.

The aim of these forty-two essays is to focus on the education of the presidents of the United States. More than three hundred illustrations with detailed captions are included. Each illustration elucidates an aspect of that president's education. Most are being published for the first time.

As with other presidential comparisons, no clear pattern emerges from their varied educations. However, most presidents from Washington through Wilson had a form of a classical education that included Bible study. Of the twenty-five pre-1900 presidents, sixteen experienced some formal higher education. Lincoln was self-educated, as were Jackson, Van Buren, Taylor, Fillmore, Andrew Johnson, and Grover Cleveland. William Henry Harrison attended medical school and James Garfield studied for the ministry.

All seventeen presidents since 1900, with the exception of Harry Truman, attended college. These colleges vary from Harding's bankrupt Ohio Central and its three instructors to the prestigious schools of Harvard, Yale, and Princeton. Hoover majored in geology at Stanford and Lyndon Johnson was trained as an elementary school teacher at a rural Texas college. Eisenhower graduated from West Point and Jimmy Carter from Annapolis. Woodrow Wilson is the only president to hold an earned doctorate degree. And, with the exception of Taft and Wilson, almost all seventeen presidents since 1900 were average students.

Collectively, these essays and illustrations are also a microcosm of American education since the 1750s. Teachers, tutors, parents, relatives, textbooks, novels, nonfiction, and the Bible—each had an important part in the education of the presidents, and therefore in shaping American history.

—Fred L. Israel

George Washington
Chapter One

No American is more completely misunderstood than George Washington. To his contemporaries, Washington—commander of the tattered colonial army (1775–1783), chairman of the Constitutional Convention (1787), and first president of the United States (1789–1797)—was indisputably first in war, first in peace, and first in the hearts of his countrymen. Thomas Jefferson spoke for the nation in 1792 when he urged Washington to seek a second term. "The confidence of the whole Union is centered in you," he told his chief. After Washington's death in 1799, Jefferson wrote, "Never did nature and fortune combine more perfectly to make a man great, and to place him in…an everlasting remembrance." Washington was the first leader in some 2,000 years to relinquish great power once he had held it. And he did it twice—both as a general at the end of the Revolutionary War and as president, stepping down from office after two terms.

But Americans were not satisfied with the realities—glorious though they were—of Washington's life. They wanted a flawless hero. And, mainly because of Mason Weems's apocryphal biography published in 1800, Washington soon came to be regarded as a demigod. Weems (1759–1825), an Episcopal clergyman, wrote *The Life and Memorable Actions of George Washington*. With the exception of the Bible, this ultra-fictionalized biography was the bestseller of its day and held its own through over seventy accredited and varying editions, including five in German. In its fifth edition, the best known of Weems's tales appeared in book form—the story of the destructive six-year-old boy with a hatchet who chops down a cherry tree, then confesses the deed to his confronting father. "With the sweet face of youth brightened with the inexpressible charm of all-conquering truth, he bravely cried out, 'I can't tell a lie, Pa; you know I can't tell a lie. I did cut it with my hatchet,'" wrote Weems. In the book, the youngster's father, Augustine "Gus" Washington Sr., responds, "Run to my arms, you dearest boy….for you have paid me for it a thousand fold." Today, two centuries after this anecdote first appeared, it still remains one of the very few episodes about Washington that most Americans are able to recite— and it remains the most memorable two pages that Weems ever wrote.

"I can't tell a lie, Pa; you know I can't tell a lie. I did cut it with my hatchet."

The anecdote of young George Washington and the cherry tree became popular because it illustrated honesty, the most important virtue, which is rewarded with paternal love. Honesty, George supposedly was told by his father "is the loveliest quality of youth." However, the story was immortalized when it was included in *McGuffey's Fifth Eclectic Reader*, an elementary school text, beginning with the 1846 edition. William McGuffey bestowed unending fame on the above print when he placed it in his *Reader*. These *Readers*, first published in 1836, went through scores of editions, were revised and enlarged, and sold more than 122 million copies. Even the simplest lessons contained obvious morals. The *Readers* introduced thousands of boys and girls to the treasures of literature. Their moral and cultural influence upon children in the thirty-seven states in which they were used contributed much to the shaping of the American mind in the nineteenth century.

THE LIFE
OF
GEORGE WASHINGTON;
WITH
CURIOUS ANECDOTES,

EQUALLY HONOURABLE TO HIMSELF,
AND
EXEMPLARY TO HIS YOUNG COUNTRYMEN.

A life how useful to his country led!
How loved while living! how revered now dead!
Lisp! lisp his name, ye children yet unborn!
And with deeds your own great names adorn.

Embellished with Six Engravings.

BY M. L. WEEMS,
FORMERLY RECTOR OF MOUNT VERNON PARISH.

The author has treated this great subject with admirable "success in a new way." He turns all the actions of Washington to the encouragement of virtue by a careful application of numerous exemplifications drawn from the conduct of the founder of our Republic from his earliest life."—H. Lee, *Major General U. S. Army.*

PHILADELPHIA:
J. B. LIPPINCOTT COMPANY.
1891.

The hatchet and cherry-tree story first appeared in book form in 1806.

16   LIFE OF WASHINGTON

fond, and was constantly going about chopping everything that came in his way. One day, in the garden, where he often amused himself hacking his mother's pea-sticks, he unluckily tried the edge of his hatchet on the body of a beautiful young English cherry-tree, which he barked so terribly, that I don't believe the tree ever got the better of it. The next morning the old gentleman, finding out what had befallen his tree, which, by the by, was a great favourite, came into the house; and with much warmth asked for the mischievous author, declaring at the same time, that he would not have taken five guineas for his tree. Nobody could tell him any thing about it. Presently George and his hatchet made their appearance. "George," said his father, "do you know who killed that beautiful little cherry tree yonder in the garden?" This was a tough question; and George staggered under it for a moment; but quickly recovered himself: and looking at his father, with the sweet face of youth brightened with the inexpressible charm of all-conquering truth, he bravely cried out, "I can't tell a lie, Pa; you know I can't tell a lie. I did cut it with my hatchet."—Run to my arms, you dearest boy, cried his father in transports, run to my arms; glad am I, George, that you killed my tree; for you have paid me for it a thousand fold. Such an act of heroism in my son is more worth than a thousand trees, though blossomed with silver, and their fruits of purest gold."

It was in this way by interesting at once both his heart and head, that Mr. Washington conducted George with great ease and pleasure along the happy paths of virtue. But well knowing that his beloved charge, soon to be a man, would be left exposed to numberless temptations, both from himself and from others, his heart throbbed with the tenderest anxiety to make him acquainted with that great being, whom to know and love, is to possess the surest defence against vice, and the best of all motives to virtue and

Mason Weems invented the story that young Washington could not tell a lie. Weems had met Washington several times, the earliest being in 1787. In 1800, one year after Washington's death, Weems had the idea for a fictionalized biography of Washington. His friend Matthew Carey, who had apprenticed in Benjamin Franklin's printing shop, was a well-known Philadelphia publisher. Carey issued the first editions of Mason Weems's biography of Washington. Sales were so outstanding that Weems, the first ordained Episcopal minister in the United States, continued to offer ideas for embellishing the story in successive editions. In its fifth edition (1806), the hatchet and cherry-tree story first appeared in book form. By the 1920s, more than seventy editions of the book had been published.

For several generations, descendants of Mason Weems were asked to autograph copies of their ancestor's book. This 1891 edition of *The Life of George Washington* is autographed: "With the compliments of the great-great-great grandson of the author. Robert Weems Tansill, Jr."

George Washington was born February 22, 1732[1], in Westmoreland County, Virginia. Without a doubt, the Washington family ranked among the privileged in colonial Virginia—and from his very first biographer stories have been told of the family's happy households, although personal relations between the children and their mother, Mary Washington, were most formal. The family's wealth came from vast tobacco plantations. Young George had to have heard everywhere discussions of business ventures and of speculative enterprises. Likewise, he had to have observed the methods of cultivation of both tobacco, the staple crop of the colony, as well as of grain crops. The Washingtons owned many slaves, and the youth probably witnessed the management of the black workforce. As a young adult, Washington viewed slavery with a crass insensitivity that only his later experiences would temper into compassion. Of the nine presidents who held slaves, he was the only one to free all of them in his will.

The major part of Washington's classroom education totaled seven or eight years. It hardly went beyond what today would be considered the elementary grades. His father, and later his older half-brothers, seem to have been his teachers. According to a biographical sketch written by his friend David Humphreys, Washington also was instructed by a tutor. There is little evidence of who that man was or whether there had been more than one teacher. Mason Weems wrote that young George attended a school run by a man names Hobby; a John Hobby did in fact operate a school near Fredericksburg. Weems also noted that a "Mr. Williams, an excellent teacher," next instructed Washington in Westmoreland County. A Henry Williams did run a school there. The yearly expenses would have been a thousand pounds of tobacco for board and two hundred pounds for instruction. However, Weems's statements can neither be proved nor disproved.

David Ramsay, in his popular biography *Life of George Washington* (1807), wrote that Washington's mother Mary had a major influence on his education, but what influence she had cannot be accurately assessed. It seems, though, that she was against her eldest son attending school any distance from home. She also stopped a plan for young George to join the Royal Navy, although his friends, the wealthy and powerful Fairfax family, would certainly have used their influence to get George a position under an outstanding commander. According to Ramsay, who interviewed family members, "it is justifiable to credit her with a decided influence in the way of discipline and morals." We do know that, widowed at age thirty-five, she did not remarry. We also know she was a most possessive person and that her son was the passion of her life.[2] When Washington was commander-in-chief of the Continental Army, and later when he was president, she bitterly complained that he neglected her. She preserved Washington's childhood school

---

[1] A change in the calendar during Washington's lifetime pushed his birthdate ahead eleven days.

[2] James Thomas Flexner wrote, "Although she lived into George's second term as president, she never budged from home to take part in any triumphant moment of his career, and all her comments that have been recorded…show her deprecating her son's achievements." (*George Washington*, vol. 1, pp. 19–20.) This evaluation does not contradict "that her son was the passion of her life."

copybooks, his earliest surviving writings. These are an indispensable source for studying the future president's education.

In later life, Washington complained his "defective education" prevented him from writing an autobiography. He always was a poor speller but Jefferson and Madison were no better. He would almost never discuss his education. One biographer noted that Washington "spelled like a gentleman—and the gentlemen of those early days were not good spellers." Yet his school exercises record instruction that was almost entirely practical. The earliest school papers have a 1741 date—he was then nine—and clearly are the work of a boy who had already learned to read, write, and do basic arithmetic. The bulk of the surviving papers date from 1744 to 1748. In total, three hundred and thirteen pages exist; they are loosely bound in four volumes and are held by the Manuscript Division of the Library of Congress.[3]

Washington's school notebooks reveal a practical education. Nearly half of the pages are exercises in mathematics—many of calculations in geometry and trigonometry, essential to understand land surveying. About fifty pages deal with practical land surveying problems. There are also lessons in which Washington had to copy lease and indenture forms, contracts, and deeds. There are pages of account keeping and of "ciphering" or handwriting exercises. At least ten pages deal with configurations of the stars and geography, both essential for navigation. All of these subjects were advantageous for a member of the Virginia gentry and essential for a plantation owner. Lacking among the notebooks is any instruction in the humanities.

When Gus Washington died in 1743, plans for young George's education changed. The eleven-year-old would not be able to follow his father and his two older half-brothers to Appleby Grammar School in Cumbria, England. (The school, founded by royal charter in 1574, is still in existence.) Instead, the next half-dozen years of Washington's life were spent living with his mother, his many relatives in Westmoreland County, and at Mount Vernon, home of his elder half-brother Lawrence.

During this period, Washington wrote in his copybook one of the most interesting documents of his education—the one hundred and ten maxims he called "Rules of Civility and Decent Behavior in Company and Conversation." They cover ten handwritten pages. (His handwriting had evolved from a childhood scrawl to a sprawling legible script.) This exercise had the most formidable influence on Washington's character. The rules, sort of a middle ground between crudeness and pomposity, were guidelines for gentlemanly good behavior—every action done in company ought to be with some sign of respect to those that are present (number one); in the presence of others, sing not to yourself with a humming noise nor drum with your fingers or feet (number two); if you cough, sleep, sigh or yawn, do it not loud but privately (number five); sleep not when others speak (number six); spit not into the fire (number nine); when you sit down, keep your feet firm and even; without putting one on the other or crossing them (number ten); kill no vermin, or

[3] The Washington Papers consist of over four hundred volumes of manuscripts, more than 75,000 pages. They were purchased from the family by the U.S. government between 1834 and 1849 for $45,000.

This University of Pennsylvania mandamus conferred the honorary Doctor of Laws Degree on George Washington, July 4, 1783, for "the establishment of Peace and the security of those important interests which were involved in the fate of the War." *Mandamus* is a Latin word that literally means "we command." In this instance, the Board of Trustees authorized the degree to be conferred on Washington. The school, founded in 1740 as the College and Academy of Philadelphia, became in 1765 with the establishment of the first medical school in America, the oldest university in the nation. Honorary degrees date back to medieval universities, a recognition of distinction without regard to academic attainment.

At about age twelve, Washington wrote in his copybook one of the most interesting documents of his education—the one hundred and ten "Rules of Civility and Decent Behavior and Conversation." They cover ten pages. His handwriting had evolved from a childhood scrawl to a sprawling legible script. This exercise had a great influence on Washington's character.

At the top, in Washington's handwriting, are the first twelve rules. Summarized in modern English, the future president is writing: treat everyone with respect; be considerate; do not embarrass others; when you speak, be concise; and do not draw attention to yourself through rude behavior.

On the right is the final of the ten pages, on which rules one hundred and four to one hundred and ten are listed. The one hundred and seventh rule advises to show interest in others' conversation but never talk when your mouth is filled with food. The final rule, "Labor to keep alive in your breast that little spark of celestial fire called conscience," means don't allow yourself to become jaded or cynical.

Washington practiced these rules as others follow the tenets of a religion. "There was a decided strain of romance in the makeup of George Washington," wrote biographer John C. Fitzpatrick, "and it was precisely to this romantic strain that these rules strongly appealed."

fleas, lice, ticks in the sight of others (number thirteen), keep your nails clean and short (number fifteen); be no flatterer (number seventeen); to the one who is your equal, or not much inferior, you are to give the chief place in your lodging (number thirty-two); when you reprove another, be unblamable yourself (number forty-eight); play not the peacock (number fifty-four); think before you speak (number seventy-three); rinse not your mouth in the presence of others (number one hundred and one). About twenty of the rules governed good table manners—"Put not your meat to your mouth with your knife....Neither spit forth the stones of any fruit pie upon a dish nor cast anything under the table....Talk not with meat in your mouth." Washington, as he groomed himself into a gentleman, memorized these maxims and practiced them throughout his life. For him, they became the civil religion that he faithfully followed. (Note that not one of these "gentlemen's rules of civility" deal with the humane treatment of a slave!)

Until the 1890s, it was assumed that Washington had composed the "rules of civility." Researchers then found that similar rules had been prepared in the 1590s by an order of French Jesuits as guide for young noblemen. Translations of the Jesuit rules subsequently appeared in both Latin and English, and may have been copied by Washington. Others have pointed out that the rules closely resemble popular courtesy books published in London during the early eighteenth century. For example, Richard Allestree's *Gentleman's Calling* and *Ladies Calling* went through many editions. These two volumes provided those rising in English society— particularly the crass new mercantile elite—with needed pointers about social behavior. Probably, either Washington's father or one of his two half-brothers purchased a book that included the rules during their student days in England. (Augustine Jr. had returned from Appleby in June 1742, shortly before Washington began writing out the "rules of civility.") It is also possible that Washington's polished half-brother Lawrence, who took an interest in Washington's education, lent him the book containing this gentleman's code. In any event, these rules of English upper-class decorum seemed appropriate to the Virginia society in which Washington lived—a society of wealthy families living opulently on their great plantations. They also defined Washington's conduct for the rest of his life.

John C. Fitzpatrick, the compiler and editor of *The Writings of George Washington* (thirty-seven volumes), wrote that Washington copied the "rules of civility" around 1744, when George was about twelve. This was the year after the death of Augustine Washington Sr., who had a large extended family, and, apparently, the implications of his complex, detailed, and most equitable will were more at the forefront than was the depth and period of mourning. Washington had a distant and deferential relationship with his father. It lacked emotion and feeling.

Washington's childhood idol was his half-brother Lawrence, who was about fourteen years his elder. As a result of Lawrence's long and careful schooling in England, he returned to Virginia a young gentleman with grace and manners that captivated young George. Lawrence was carefully courteous and deferential to the rich and powerful he came to know. He preferred horses to books. His greatest gifts were social. He was extremely cultured but probably gave the impression of a wider learning than he had mastered. In today's vernacular, Lawrence would be called a "social snob." A little more than two months after their father's death, Lawrence married into the Fairfax family, one of the wealthiest families not only in Virginia but in the American colonies. This assured Lawrence's place in the front rank of socially conscious Virginia society.

The Fairfaxes of Virginia lived like medieval feudal lords. The family owned more than five million acres in perpetuity between the Potomac and Rappahannock Rivers—a 1649 grant made by the future King Charles II—that the proprietor could do with as he pleased. Lawrence's father-in-law, Colonel William Fairfax, was a cousin and agent of Thomas, sixth Lord Fairfax, the great proprietor. William was George's favorite Fairfax: he took a strong liking to the colonel, and the older Fairfax reciprocated. He encouraged Washington to ride and hunt, and taught him how to dress in the latest fashion. It was the colonel, as well as Lawrence Washington, who introduced young George to Roman history and literature and to English aristocratic manners. Washington later wrote that of all the Fairfaxes he was most indebted to the colonel, who became his second father and his role model—and to the colonel, George had become like a son. In this atmosphere, George had every reason to consult his handwritten "rules of civility."

Around 1747, when young Washington was about fifteen, Thomas, sixth Lord Fairfax settled in Virginia. Biographers describe this fifty-four-year-old as a somewhat eccentric, crusty character, even a recluse and misogynist. Fairfax was an Oxford graduate, an outstanding hound-breeder and foxhunter, and the first true English nobleman George Washington ever saw. He also was the first English lord ever to come live in America, and he set the priorities and social standards in the Fairfax world. To visit the Fairfaxes was similar to visiting an ultra-aristocratic English family. Their plantation had drawing rooms, a music room, an enormous dining room and a grand library filled with guests dressed in the latest London fashions. Because of the Fairfax influence, George now read more. He read the first one hundred and forty-three issues of Joseph Addison's and Richard Steele's *Spectator*, which was filled with the wit and politics of English society. Addison and Steele were fond of using classical quotations and apparently Washington memorized many that he freely used in his later correspondence. Washington also learned about the London theater from the latest issues of *Gentleman's Magazine*. Fairfax had a fetish for clothing and annually purchased the best and the latest London styles—but he did not wear them, preferring "that rougher costume which better corresponded to his out-of-door habits." His Lordship could not be questioned and he did what he pleased.

Fairfax's biographers agree that he enjoyed the company of young men. Until his marriage, George Washington shared his time between the Fairfax estates, his brother's home at Mount Vernon, and his mother's plantation. When Lord Fairfax

These are the things which once possess'd Will make a life that's truly bless'd…

This prophetic poem appears in George Washington's "school exercise book." He was about nine years of age when he copied the poem from an issue of the London publication *Gentleman's Magazine*. (The spelling and punctuation have been modernized.)

> These are the things which once possess'd
> Will make a life that's truly bless'd:
> A good estate on healthy soil
> Not got by vice, nor yet by toil:
> Round a warm fire, a pleasant joke.
> With chimney ever free from smoke:
> A strength entire, a sparkling bowl,
> A quiet wife, a quiet soul.
> A mind as well as body whole:
> Prudent simplicity, constant friends,
> A diet which no art commends:
> A merry night without much drinking,
> A happy thought without much thinking:
> Each night by quiet sleep made short,
> A will to be but what thou art:
> Possess'd of these, all else defy,
> And either wish nor fear to die.

At the bottom of the page are instructions on how to keep ink from freezing and moulding which Washington copied from the 1727 London edition of George Fisher's *The Instructor: or, Young Man's Best Companion:* "Put a few drops of brandy or other spirits into it and it will not freeze and to hinder its moulding put a little salt therein."

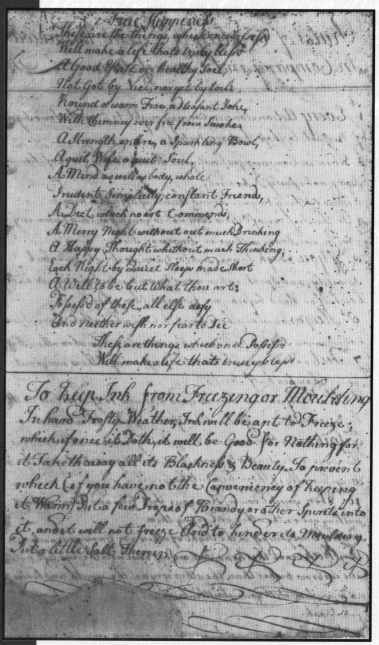

talked of battles and sieges and of an officer's gallant service, he probably made a soldier's life appear attractive to George. In his drawing rooms, Fairfax laid plans for opening up the vast new Virginia frontier. He had grown fond of tall, elegantly mannered George, now sixteen, and gave him the opportunity to have a fascinating experience—to be part of a surveying group that mapped the remotest parts of the Fairfax lands for new towns and settlements. This was George's farthest journey from home, a journey that included his first contact with the western wilderness. When Lord Fairfax died in 1781, Washington was genuinely moved. It is ironic that George Washington, the leader of the rebellion, learned his social graces from the Fairfaxes who educated him in an aristocratic lifestyle, the antithesis of the American Revolution.

Obviously, Washington absorbed ideas from the society in which he lived. Within the Virginia tidewater area, that low-lying coastal plain where the rivers rise and fall with the ocean tides, there were no less than eight strata of society. At the top were the landed proprietors (among them the Washingtons), while at the bottom were the black slaves; both groups were of immutable station. Other classes were small farmers, merchants, sailors, frontier people, indentured servants, and convict servants who worked on the plantations.

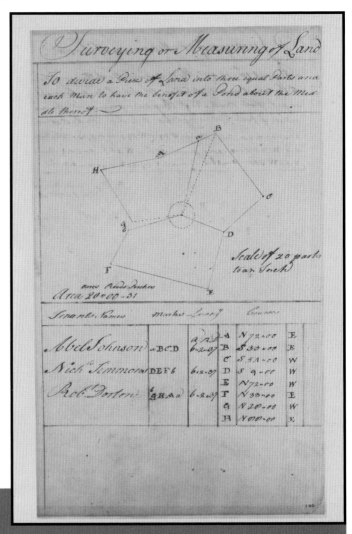

Washington completed the surveying problems shown on these pages when he was between fifteen and sixteen years old. The problems solved show that Washington had studied geography, geometric constructions, and the zodiacal configuration of the stars. "Surveying or Measuring of Land" account for thirty-nine of the one hundred and twenty pages in Washington's last extant notebook.

Washington's formal education ended when he was about sixteen. Only the surveying problems had carried him beyond what would today be considered the elementary school level.

In 1748, Thomas, sixth Lord Fairfax, gave sixteen-year-old Washington the opportunity to be part of a surveying group that mapped the remotest parts of the extensive Fairfax lands for new towns and settlements. During the thirty-one day expedition across the Blue Ridge Mountains, conducted in windy March and early April—ideal surveying weather, as tree leaves had to be down to sight through the theodolite—Washington studied the methods of experienced surveyors and wrote the field notes as they dictated them.

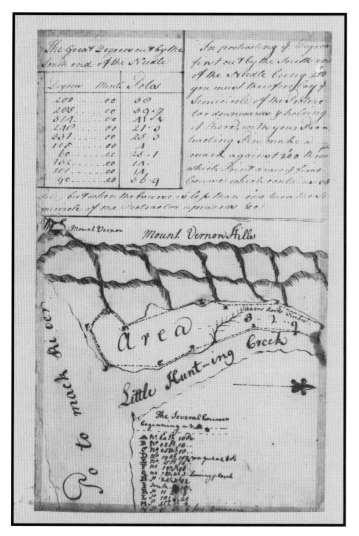

Everyone assumed that there would always be distinctions of social rank, an arrangement that seemed perfectly ordinary and proper at the time.

The planter class, an elite group, kept close ties with England and copied the manners of its aristocracy. Many lived in great Georgian mansions. They filled well-proportioned rooms with the finest imported furniture or hired artisans to carry out the designs of foreign cabinetmakers. Contemporary artists painted the gentry in all their imported finery. From the 1730s to the 1750s, the price of Virginia tobacco soared and rising profits made the planters' land more valuable. Washington doubtless understood the talk amongst his elders concerning surveying and patenting of western lands, of farming and horses, and of life along the Potomac, Rappahannock, and the James Rivers. Beyond these lands was the great, open, unclaimed Valley of the Ohio—with the promise of a fortune for young men of enterprise and courage.

From 1732 to the conclusion of the French and Indian War in 1763—that is, the first thirty years of Washington's life—nothing really happened politically that could have anticipated the American Revolution and the emergence of the "founding father" of a new nation, the first in modern history to successfully break away from its mother country. No person could have predicted how Washington or how any of his contemporaries would react to the political situation which subsequently developed. Washington's formal education was poor compared to the educations of such Patriot leaders as John Adams and Thomas Jefferson. He had not read the classics. He never learned a foreign language. He did not study law. He was uninterested in science. He was not intellectually inquisitive. However, by his early twenties, Washington's complicated character had emerged—he was moral, just, patient, ambitious, amicable, tenacious, and had the ability to make and maintain friendships. His responses were certain when his personal code of principles was involved. Even those who opposed him politically spoke generously of his fair mindedness and his sterling integrity. However, nothing in his education could have prepared him for the revolutionary events that followed.

—Fred L. Israel

John Adams
C h a p t e r   T w o

Fifteen-year-old John Adams sat motionless on his horse, shocked at what he had been told. John had been ready to ride north from Braintree, Massachusetts, to Harvard College, outside Boston, where he was to take his entrance exams to continue his education. He had expected his teacher, Joseph Marsh, to travel with him and to be there through the testing on that June morning of 1751. John had just learned that Mr. Marsh felt sick and was afraid to travel. He would have to go alone.

The future second President of the United States was so unsure of his ability to pass the test that he almost turned his horse around to ride the short distance back home. Then John thought of how upset and disappointed his father would be if he failed to take the exams. He also realized that his father might be angry with Mr. Marsh for not going. John forced himself to turn his horse toward Boston and begin the journey by himself.

The day grew overcast with dark skies that threatened rain as John traveled the fifteen miles to Boston. From time to time he could see the slate gray Massachusetts Bay beyond the hills to his right. Finally, John crossed the Charles River and approached the four buildings that made up Harvard College in 1751. With some fear and uncertainty, John talked with Harvard President Edward Holyoke and several Harvard tutors. Then he was given an essay in English to be translated into Latin.

The ride back to Braintree was far different for John than his trip to Harvard. He had passed the exams and been accepted into Harvard as part of the class of 1755. John was lighthearted and enthusiastic on the way home, knowing that his father would be pleased with his success. Only about one half of one percent of young men went on to college in that time. Before long, John Adams passed by the Blue Hills, which were not far from his family's fifty-acre farm. It was on that farm that he had been born October 30, 1735, and where his education had begun.

Braintree (now Quincy) was a small village of approximately 1,500 people and a number of buildings, including a schoolhouse, a gristmill, a village store, several taverns, and a church. The Adams's farm was built right beside the shore road from Boston to Plymouth, at the base of Penn's Hill.

The Harvard University Archives

The Harvard University Archives are unique because they contain a continuous record of the oldest institution of higher learning in the United States. Many of the early college records were kept in bound volumes. These have been preserved intact.

In the 1930s, Samuel Eliot Morison compiled an "Inventory of the Harvard University Archives, to 1800." It remains the outstanding explanation and inventory of the archives for the seventeenth and eighteenth centuries. Morison's essay describes the record organization of the college—for example, "The College Books," "Corporation Records," "Overseers, Records," "Harvard College Papers," "President's Papers," "Professorship Papers," "Treasurer's Records," etc. In 1939, the Harvard Corporation established the Harvard University Archives as a unit within the University Library. The Archives mission was greatly enhanced by its move in 1976 from the top floor of Widener Library into much larger quarters in the Pusey Library. These archival records are an indispensable source for understanding the history of the college.

John Adams's student years at Harvard College, 1751–55, occurred in the middle of the thirty-two year administration of President Edward Holyoke (1737–69). This was a period of prosperity and progress for the college. Holyoke, who had been born in 1689, previously had been pastor of the Marblehead, Massachusetts, Congregational Church for twenty-one years. As president, Holyoke lessened the Calvinist dominance in the Harvard College curriculum. Textbooks he thought dated were replaced with newer works. Scottish philosopher David Fordyce's *Elements of Moral Philosophy* (1754) and John Locke's *An Essay Concerning Human Understanding* (1689) became required reading. Scientific instruction was modernized. Oratory was encouraged through regularly scheduled student debates. Academic awards were given to outstanding students for the first time in the college's history.

Holyoke was instrumental in the hiring of younger and less religiously dogmatic instructors, among them John Winthrop. Winthrop, a direct descendant of the colonial leader John Winthrop (1587/88–1649), was elected the second Hollis Professor of Mathematics and Natural Philosophy in 1738 at the age of twenty-four. Winthrop was the first important scientist and productive scholar on the teaching staff of Harvard College. In 1751, with Holyoke's approval, Winthrop introduced "elements of fluxions,"—now known as differential and integral calculus—into the Harvard mathematical curriculum. In addition to teaching, Winthrop also gave public lectures and demonstrations in physical science. His research work, mainly in the field of astronomy, was carried out over a period of forty years, during which Winthrop came to be considered one of the outstanding scholars in the nation. Winthrop was young John Adams's favorite professor. Adams ecstatically recorded in his diary the clear night when he first gazed through Professor Winthrop's telescope at the satellites of Jupiter.

Nonetheless, during Adams's time at Harvard the college's curriculum was very similar to the Harvard of a century before. Latin and Greek were essential for all applicants. Entrance examinations were oral, except that the student usually had to write a Latin essay to test his skill in "making" Latin. All students were male. Student numbers had increased under President Holyoke but the largest graduating class before the American Revolution, that of 1771, numbered sixty-three. It was not until 1810 that another graduating class reached that figure. (Adams's graduating class of 1755 numbered twenty-seven.)

Most Harvard students were the sons of merchants, magistrates, and ministers from New England. Most students came from eastern Massachusetts and New Hampshire. Not a single New Yorker appears on the Harvard registration rolls between 1737 and 1790. About one student from the West Indies came to Harvard every two years or so from 1737 on. The median age of freshmen entering the college rose from a low of little over fifteen years in 1741 to seventeen years in 1769.

Inventories submitted by students burned out of their rooms after a 1764 fire list tables; chairs; feather beds; pictures and looking glasses; issues of leading London magazines such as Joseph Addison and Richard Steele's *The Spectator* and *The Tatler* and copies of England's popular *Gentleman's Magazine* (the periodical that gave the word "magazine" to the genre); books of popular plays; clothing; wigs and crisping irons; chafing dishes; tea sets; pipes and tobacco; rum and other liquors; corkscrews; and one Bible.

Harvard was noted for its outstanding classical education. It was this classical education that assisted Adams and his classmates later in politics and statesmanship. Eight of the fifty-six signers of the Declaration of Independence graduated from Harvard between 1740 and 1762. Each had been taught by Edward Holyoke. As these men became involved with the events that led to the American Revolution, they saw lessons for their own time in the writings of Plutarch and the orations of Cicero and Demosthenes, and they understood the logic of Plato's *Republic* and Aristotle's *Politics*.

The Harvard University Archives are unique because they contain a continuous record of the oldest institution of higher learning in the United States.

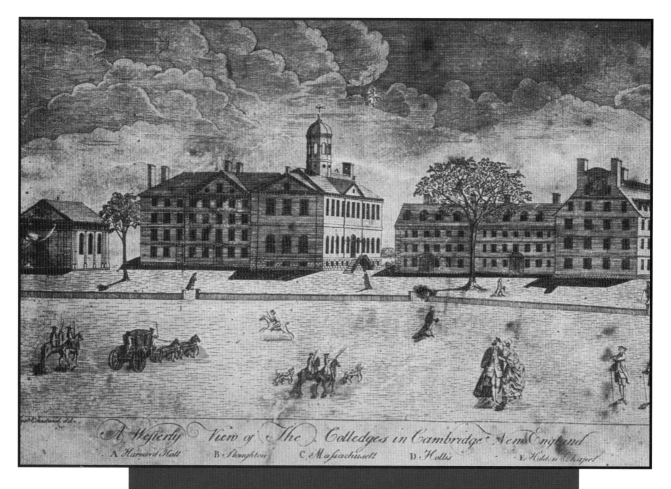

A Westerly View of The Colledges in Cambridge New England
A Harvard Hall   B Stoughton   C Massachusett   D Hollis   v. Holden Chapel

Old Harvard Hall, where John Adams studied, burned down on the night of January 24, 1764. It was replaced by the building with the steeple in the center of this 1767 drawing. The drawing was done by Joseph Chadwick and engraved by Paul Revere. It is the earliest engraving that shows Hollis Hall and the new Harvard Hall.

In 1764, Hollis Hall (the second building from left) was completed to house students because of growing enrollment. It was named after the English family that had sent continuous benefices to Harvard for almost fifty years.

To ensure that college property was kept in good condition—and to facilitate collection of fines for broken windows and other damages—Harvard was divided into districts. Students or tutors were assigned to inspect each district. The quarterly District Reports preserved in the Harvard Archives give a great deal of information about the condition of buildings and the occupants of college dormitory rooms. These reports ended in the mid-nineteenth century.

The Massachusetts Bay Colony, where John Adams was born, had been founded by Puritans in 1630. They were English settlers who firmly believed that the duty of humankind was to serve God. They wanted to see the Christian Church purified and restored to the condition they believed it had been in the time of Jesus. Because Puritans felt that the best way to do this was to know and obey the Bible, learning to read was essential for everyone. They wanted the whole population to be able to gain a basic understanding of the biblical Scriptures. Puritans had no concept of a separation between church and state; instead they believed religion and government should work together to create a righteous and just society.

The Puritan determination to educate all their citizens was seen early in the colony's history. Only five years after the founding of Massachusetts, the first Latin Grammar School was established in Boston. Just a year later, in 1636, Harvard College was begun for the purpose of training men for the Christian ministry. The Puritan leaders believed that the churches of New England needed an educated clergy. An act was passed in Massachusetts in 1647 that required every town of one hundred families or more to provide free grammar school education for their children. By 1750, about 75 percent of males and 65 percent of females in New England could read and write. That was the highest literacy rate in colonial America.

The Adams' family had settled in Massachusetts one hundred years before John was born. His father, Deacon John Adams (so-called because he was a deacon in the local church), had married Susanna Boylston of Brookline, a small village near Boston. Deacon John and Susanna had three sons: John was the eldest, followed by Peter and Elihu. Deacon John was a farmer and shoemaker. Though he had never been to college, he wanted his eldest son to have a college education. It was his desire that John become a minister like his uncle. Deacon John's other two sons would join him working on the farm.

John Adams's first taste of studying occurred in his own home. Most literate parents in those days educated their children in basic principles before they were five; John's parents began to teach him his ABC's and the fundamentals of reading. Their interest in education seems to have run in the family. Deacon John's mother, Hannah, was described as a person who had more books than was usual in those days, especially for a woman. She was a diligent reader, as was Deacon John. It would be years, though, before young John would discover this same interest for himself.

After home schooling by his parents, John continued on in his education by attending what was then called a "dame school." At about six years of age, children would attend a school in the home of a neighborhood woman, a "dame." In John Adams's case, that woman was Mrs. Belcher, the mother of another deacon in the family's local congregational church. For two years John left his home each morning and crossed the road to Mrs. Belcher's kitchen, where she taught the neighborhood children.

One primary educational tool from which John learned at the dame school was called a hornbook. This was a wooden frame, shaped like a paddle, with a sheet of paper containing letters of the alphabet or simple words mounted on it. The hornbook had a long handle, so John could hold it while studying. The frame was covered with a piece of transparent horn from a sheep or ox to keep the sheet from getting stained. A hole was cut into the handle and a rope inserted, so John could carry it on his belt or around his neck when it was not in use.

A second important educational tool was one used in New England schools throughout the eighteenth century—the *New England Primer*. The primer is believed to have been created by Benjamin Harris, a London printer who came to Boston around 1686. The *New England Primer* began with written prayers and then continued with the alphabet and words with increasing levels of difficulty. This was followed by rhymes to remember the alphabet such as

In ADAM'S Fall
We sinned all.
Heaven to find;
The BIBLE Mind.

There were rhymes for each letter of the alphabet from A to Z. Next in the *New England Primer* were poems, hymns, and a lengthy catechism, which was a summary of religious teaching in the form of questions and answers. The purpose of the primer was to give children instruction in both their letters and in religion.

When John was about eight, he completed the dame school and began attending the Braintree Latin School. This was a public school run at the time by Joseph Cleverly, a graduate of Harvard College and a reader at the Episcopal Church in Braintree. The heart of the curriculum in the school was Latin, the foundation for many other languages and a necessary tool for higher education in the eighteenth century. John also learned Greek, the language in which the New Testament had originally been written.

Two other important subjects studied at the Latin school were rhetoric and logic. The aim of rhetoric was to teach a student to write and speak with ease and confidence. Because Latin schools were designed to prepare young men for Harvard, it was almost certain that those who attended college would one day become pastors, teachers, or lawyers. These were all professions in which writing and public speaking were important. Logic was equally necessary, Puritans believed, because it helped students develop rational, sound thinking.

It was under Mr. Cleverly's teaching that young John Adams almost gave up on school. John believed that even though his schoolmaster knew a lot, he was a lazy teacher and did little to encourage his students to want to learn. John increasingly disliked the classroom and tried to avoid going to school. He had always been a person who loved the outdoors, so he often skipped class and went out to play. Because he lived near the ocean, he would swim in the quiet bays near his home, fly kites in the breezes off the bay, and play marbles. In the winter John would ice skate and walk through the fields. Above all, he loved hunting and liked to sit on the

In their meeting of April 29, 1755, the Harvard Overseers approved plans for the class of 1755's commencement. John Adams was in this class, along with twenty-six other students.

The Overseers also approved recommendations for curriculum and financial changes. Mention is made of rent money from a farm in Norfolk, England, donated to Harvard by a London merchant named Pennoyer in 1670. These rents were paid to Harvard College until 1903 when the Overseers ordered the property sold.

In the middle paragraph, the Overseers approved an inquiry into recent student disturbances. Judging from these records and those of the faculty, the most frequent student disturbances involved "indecent tumultuous noises" and "hollowing" or "huzzas" in the Yard late at night—sometimes followed by throwing a brick through a tutor's window.

On this list of Overseers are family names that had been associated with Harvard for several generations—Foxcroft, Willard, Hutchinson, Sewall, Chauncey, Whoolwright, and Pemberton.

At the March 24 meeting, a student was excused for one week to assist his father in rebuilding their house that was "consumed by fire."

Pages from Harvard faculty records for 1769. The faculty voted to excuse students so they might return home to recuperate from an illness or for another specific purpose. For example, at the March 24 meeting, a student was excused for one week to assist his father in rebuilding their house that was "consumed by fire." At the October 9 meeting (right) an inquiry was held into an effigy of a tutor that was "suspended from a tree on the North side of the Holden Chapel." When college authorities cut the effigy down, a "number of students" acted in a "riotous manner with indecent and tumultuous noises to the great disruption of the college."

ground for hours watching for crows and squirrels to shoot. Sometimes he carried his gun to school in the morning and hid it in a neighbor's barn. Then, as early as he could, John slipped away from class, picked up the gun, and headed for the woods.

In spite of his feelings toward his teacher, John seemed to have an inborn desire to learn. John believed that Mr. Cleverly did not spend enough time in class to cover mathematics adequately, so he managed to get his own copy of the book used at the Latin school, Edward Cocker's *Decimal Arithmetic*, and studied it at home by himself. He went through the entire book and surpassed the other students in his class.

One day John begged his father to let him leave school and join his two brothers on the farm. Deacon John couldn't understand why his oldest son was more enthusiastic about work and sports than about studies. He decided to show John how hard life was as a farmer. The next morning the two went off to spend the entire day in the marshes gathering thatch. That night, though John was wet and tired, he still wanted to work on the family farm instead of continuing in school. His father didn't give in, however, and the very next day John was back at school.

Finally, when Adams was fourteen, he told his father that his real problem was with his schoolmaster. He asked Deacon John to approach Joseph Marsh, minister of the Congregational parish of Braintree, who ran a private Latin school near the Adams's farm. At the time, Marsh accepted only students from other towns, who boarded with him. John wanted his father to plead with Mr. Marsh to let him attend his private school. The next morning, the first words John heard from his father were, "I've persuaded Mr. Marsh to take you—and you must go this day!"

Marsh was able to inspire John and earn his respect. For the first time, young John began to enjoy the classroom. In less than two years, Marsh was convinced that young Adams was ready to take the entrance exams for Harvard. John was prepared for the next step in his education.

When Adams arrived at Harvard in the late summer of 1751, the college had undergone many changes. The college was named after a young minister, John Harvard, and had originally existed primarily to prepare ministers for Puritan congregations in New England. By 1708, however, when the college elected its first non-clergyman president, Harvard had already moved away from Puritanism. The curriculum continued to broaden through the eighteenth century, and more of the school's graduates became lawyers or doctors than ministers. There was more critical thinking even when it came to discussing theological ideas.

John Adams loved his years at Harvard. He once wrote that it was there that he experienced a "growing curiosity, a love of books and a fondness for study, which dissipated all my inclination for sports, and even for the society of ladies." He read constantly and concentrated on mathematics and philosophy. His knowledge of Latin, Greek, rhetoric, and logic grew deeper. When John entered Harvard, each class had a tutor who would work with them through their college years. Professor Joseph Mayhew was tutor for the class of 1755; he had been one of the men who had examined John for admittance to Harvard.

Adams and his twenty-three fellow classmates had a regular routine they followed the entire school year. They got up before sunrise, said prayers and ate breakfast, then attended classes from 8 A.M. to 5 P.M. with a break for lunch. There were lectures by professors and, often twice a week, debates on issues prepared by their class tutors. After dinner, the students would study until bedtime. The school year began in late August and continued until the end of December, when they were given a five-week winter break. School would then resume until the end of June, when they would have a six-week summer vacation before beginning their next year.

One powerful incentive that moved John Adams to learn was the presence of so many good students in his class. He was competitive and wanted to do better than his classmates. Throughout his four years, he never envied the gifts of fellow students but enjoyed the challenge he received from them. Their friendships caused John to pursue his studies with greater determination than ever. Many of his classmates went on to notable careers. One of these was Samuel Locke, who eventually became the president of Harvard. Another was John Wentworth, who went from college to become the last royal governor of New Hampshire. Tristram Dalton, also in the class of 1755, became one of the first U.S. Senators from Massachusetts.

Adams entered college with his father's expectation that he would become a minister. However, as the years at Harvard passed, events caused John to consider other options. During his junior year, John learned that his pastor in Braintree, Lemuel Bryant, was in a dispute with members of his congregation. Some congregants were critical of Reverend Bryant's preaching and his actions. John read published arguments on both sides and saw much narrowness of opinion. He seriously questioned whether he wanted to pursue a career that might put him in the same kind of conflict.

At this same time, Adams joined a group of students who spent evenings in readings and discussion. When he once read aloud some dramatic material, many of his fellow students told him he had a gift for public speaking and urged him to consider becoming a lawyer. Something responded inside of John, and he began to think seriously about law as a profession. He reasoned that his parents would accept a change in his career. He was certain that he could convince his father of the logic of such a decision, and he knew his mother had no great desire for him to become a pastor.

The real obstacle that stood in Adams's way was a lack of money. There were no law schools in America in the eighteenth century, so the only way to become a lawyer was to study as an apprentice under an established lawyer. In order to do that, John would have to pay a fee to a lawyer to tutor him and somehow find the money for his room, board, and necessities. It would take him at least two years before he would be ready to practice law himself. John Adams knew that he could not ask his father for any more financial assistance.

In his last year of Harvard, Adams decided to become a teacher while he grappled with the final choice for his lifetime career. Before graduation, he accepted a position as Latin master in a grammar school in Worcester, sixty miles west of

Harvard student room assignments, circa 1754. John Adams lived in Massachusetts Hall, Room 31 (his entry is on line nine). Adams described the shared room as being the "lowermost northwest chamber" of the building. Among Adams's classmates listed on this room directory were John Hancock, Thomas Sparhawk (with whom Adams roomed in their senior year), and Joseph Stockbridge, the wealthiest student in the class.

Boston, where he moved after he received his bachelor of arts degree in 1755. Once there, the town boarded him for three weeks, and then Adams found a room in the home of a prominent doctor, Dr. Nahum Willard. One incentive for Adams to live with the Willards was their large library. He realized he would have access to these many books as a border in the Willard home.

Adams's move to Worcester was a difficult one. After the stimulating environment of college, he found the townspeople to be less interesting. Worcester was about the size of Braintree, but much more isolated. He also found teaching frustrating because his students seemed dull. Adams would often select the smartest student to lead the class while he sat at his desk reading or writing.

However, he was able to spend many evenings discussing ideas with leading citizens of Worcester. Of particular interest at the time were new religious ideas flooding the colonies. Adams read a theological book, Thomas Morgan's *The Moral Philosopher*, and argued over its theology with his new friends. He also pored over many of Dr. Willard's medical books and for a time thought about medicine as a career.

Adams's uncertainties about his future continued. At times he disliked himself for his inability to make up his mind. Yet, when he began to visit the courts in Worcester and listen to gifted lawyers, Adams found his interest in law growing stronger. Finally, he decided to make law his career. As a result, he entered into the final stage of his formal education. At the end of the summer of 1756, Adams contacted a Worcester lawyer, James Putnam, about the possibility of becoming his apprentice. Mr. Putnam agreed to tutor him, and Adams moved in with the Putnam family to begin a two-year program studying law.

Adams's law education became more practical after he began attending court with Putnam to watch him in action. After a time, he began to prepare briefs— statements or summaries of Putnam's cases going to trial. Adams continued this practice of reading, discussing, visiting court, and working on briefs for two years. In October of 1758, he finished his law studies with Putnam. Through an oversight, Putnam neglected to give Adams the recommendation needed for him to practice law. So Adams introduced himself to Attorney General Jeremy Gridley, who liked him and gave him the necessary certificate and recommended him to the court. This letter of recommendation was almost equivalent to a law degree.

Adams decided to return to his parent's home because Braintree was in the Boston judicial district where he would have more opportunities than in distant Worcester. Once Adams was settled, he visited some prominent lawyers in the bustling city of Boston to seek their support and advice. He also sized up his opposition among other young lawyers in the area. He realized that some of them had influential friends who could help them advance in their careers. With that advantage over him, Adams decided to develop a plan of reading over the next few years so that he would have a greater knowledge of the law.

Adams was encouraged to continue his reading by his friend Jeremy Gridley, who allowed Adams to use his extensive library. Pointing to his books, Gridley once told Adams, "There is the secret of my eminence." John spent much time in Gridley's library, filling his mind with as much of the law as he could. He had learned to continue his own education through a consistent habit of reading.

On October 25, 1764, John Adams, who was then twenty-eight, married nineteen-year-old Abigail Smith, from the nearby town of Weymouth. Daughter of a pastor, Abigail was a remarkably well-read and intellectual woman. Like John, she loved to read and was an excellent writer. The two of them carried on a lengthy correspondence for years when John became active in politics and was gone for lengthy periods of time. John and Abigail Adams would have five children, including John Quincy Adams, the sixth president of the United States.

John and Abigail moved to Boston in 1768, where John continued his practice and became well respected among its citizens. Adams became widely known throughout the city in 1770 when he agreed to defend some British soldiers stationed in Boston who had killed some townspeople. That episode became known as the Boston Massacre. Most of the soldiers were acquitted, and though Adams was disliked at the time, his willingness to protect the innocent—no matter who they were—eventually won him great respect.

As resistance to Great Britain grew in America, John Adams became one of the most outspoken advocates for a war of independence. In 1774, Adams was a delegate from Massachusetts to the Continental Congress and headed the committee to draft the Declaration of Independence. After the colonies gained their freedom, Adams served the United States as its first American minister to Great Britain. In 1789, he was elected vice president under George Washington, and in 1797 was elected president.

After serving one term, and losing his bid for a second term to Thomas Jefferson, Adams retired to Braintree. There he had the time once again for his books and study. "Learning, he said, "is not to be obtained by chance, but must be sought after with vigor." He died on July 4, 1826, the fiftieth anniversary of the signing of the Declaration of Independence, just a few hours after the death of Thomas Jefferson. Adams was buried next to his beloved Abigail, who had died in 1818.

Perhaps John Adams's life can best be summarized by biographer David McCullough: "As his family and friends knew, Adams was both a devout Christian and an independent thinker, and he saw no conflict in that. He was hardheaded and a man of 'sensibility,' a close observer of human folly as displayed in everyday life and fired by an inexhaustible love of books and scholarly reflection."

—Bill Thompson

Thomas Jefferson
Chapter Three

"I cannot live without books," wrote Thomas Jefferson to his friend, John Adams, as both were nearing the end of their lives. As he wrote these words, Jefferson could look back on a life filled with reading and intense study. Jefferson remembered how he had developed this love of learning during his childhood in Virginia. He had acquired it first from his father, Peter, who was determined to develop his own mind in spite of his lack of formal education.

Both Thomas Jefferson and his father, Peter, were born in the southern colony of Virginia, where public education was not a high priority. Unlike some of the northern colonies, where the government insisted on providing schools for its children, Virginia authorities left education to the Anglican clergy. The Episcopalian pastors, called rectors, were expected to educate the young through sermons, classes, and personal visits. Any education beyond that was the responsibility of individual families—if they could afford to hire tutors for their children.

When Peter Jefferson was a boy, his father taught him to read and write but did not provide any other education. However, Peter was determined to educate himself, and he began to acquire books early in his life. Books were rare in Virginia then, especially on the frontier. Peter began to develop a small library that included the Bible and works by Shakespeare and other English writers. Peter learned the techniques of mapping while traveling throughout Virginia as a surveyor. Along with Joshua Fry, Peter Jefferson made the first detailed map of Virginia. It was published in 1751 and used extensively for many years.

Peter married Jane Randolph in 1739 and took her to his farm in Goochland County, near the Southwest Mountains of Virginia. He named it Shadwell in honor of his wife's birthplace in England. Peter's interest in education grew as a result of his marriage. The men of the Randolph family, who owned vast estates in Virginia, had all graduated from the College of William and Mary in Williamsburg, Virginia. When Thomas Jefferson was born on April 13, 1743, Peter was determined to educate his son and one day send him to the College of William and Mary.

The College of William and Mary

The College of William and Mary at Williamsburg, Virginia, is the second-oldest institution of higher education in the United States (after Harvard College). King William III and Queen Mary II of England chartered the college in 1693 to train Anglican clergymen and colonial civil servants. The scholastic honor society Phi Beta Kappa was organized there in 1776. Seven signers of the Declaration of Independence—including Thomas Jefferson, its author; John Marshall, the fourth chief justice of the U.S. Supreme Court; and James Monroe, later the fifth U.S. president—were college alumni, as was President John Tyler. George Washington was the college's first American chancellor (1788–99).

In March 1760, Thomas Jefferson entered the College of William and Mary. He completed his studies there two years later. His chief intellectual stimulus while a student came from his association with Dr. William Small, who held the first chair of mathematics and then that of natural philosophy (science). Small aroused in Jefferson an interest in science that was destined to persist throughout his life. The professor also introduced Jefferson to Virginia's governor, Francis Fauquier, and to George Wythe, the most noted teacher of law of his generation.

Small's appointment to William and Mary was an attempt by Governor Fauquier to break the clerical domination of the college. Small considered himself an apostle of the Enlightenment, a teacher who must pass on to his students the need to question all dogma. He remained at the college for only six years (1758–64) because of difficulties with his colleagues. His aloofness, his perceived feigned migraines, and, above all, his inborn sense of intellectual superiority caused the cancellation of his teaching contract, undoubtedly by mutual consent. Small returned to England.

Small recognized that Jefferson was uniquely talented. That a polymath of such rare quality should be at William and Mary at the right moment to teach the polymath of them all is one of the happiest coincidences in educational history.

In 1775, just before the outbreak of the American Revolution, Jefferson wrote to Small that he was sending "half of a little present he had laid by"—three dozen bottles of Madeira that had aged for eight years in the Monticello cellars. Small had no opportunity to enjoy the wine, for he had been dead for two months when Jefferson sent off the gift. Jefferson wrote nothing as an obituary, though for the rest of his life Small's name would enter again and again into his conversation and correspondence, always followed with an expression of affection, respect, and indebtedness.

"I cannot live without books," wrote Thomas Jefferson…. As he wrote these words, Jefferson could look back on a life filled with reading and intense study.

When Thomas Jefferson was born on April 13, 1743, Peter was determined to educate his son and send him to the College of William and Mary one day.

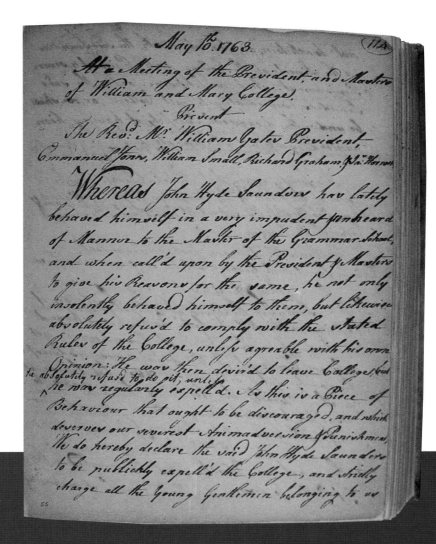

On May 10, 1763 William Small was one of four "Masters," in addition to the college president, present at a discipline hearing for John Hyde Saunders of Williamsburg. The young man had been "very impudent....to the Master of the Grammar School." He was "insolent" and "absolutely refus'd to comply with the stated Rules of the College." Saunders was expelled. Young Saunders's father had built the stables for the college. In 1772, he was awarded the contract to build "the new west wing," the first major construction undertaken at the school in forty years.

Most punishments recorded in the Faculty Minutes were imposed for drunkenness or for brawling with the local boys of Williamsburg. Extant records indicate that Small became involved in faculty discussions mainly when the purchase of scientific equipment was discussed. The Reverend William Yates, listed in this document, served as the fifth president of William and Mary (1761–68). Dumas Malone, who wrote a multi-volume biography of Jefferson, quoted John Page, Jefferson's classmate and friend, who described how they "suffered" from Yates's "arid teaching."

The earliest memory Thomas Jefferson had was from when he was two years old. Someone handed him up to a slave sitting high on one of his fathers' horses. He sat on a pillow so he could manage the long trip ahead of them. At that time the Jefferson family moved east to Tuckahoe Plantation, to run the estate owned by Peter Jefferson's wife's cousin who had died. It would be Tom's home for the next six years and where he received his first formal education.

Thomas Jefferson began the first phase of his formal education at Tuckahoe in an "English school." The Randolph and Jefferson children attended a one-room schoolhouse built on the grounds of the estate. Thomas studied along with his two older sisters, the Randolph children, and several of their cousins. Their teacher was an Anglican churchman who taught them the basics of reading, writing, and arithmetic.

As was typical in colonial days, the rector included the recitation of prayers and Bible reading in his instruction. Jefferson never took to religion, however, and was not sure about prayer. According to one story, Jefferson left the classroom one day and decided to test the power of prayer by asking for dinnertime to come quickly because he was hungry. As his life progressed, Thomas Jefferson became convinced that religion and education should be kept separate.

Peter spent much time and energy in personally developing his son's education. In the evenings, he taught Tom penmanship, insisting that he be precise and neat. Tom learned mathematics, how to keep accounts accurately, and how to work systematically. His father instilled in Tom his commitment to books, and it seems probable that Tom began reading books in his father's library even before he went to the English school at age five. Tom was taken on walks through the woods around Tuckahoe, and developed an interest in animal and plant life. Peter also began to teach his young son the basics of surveying, which had provided such a good living for him on the frontier.

Peter Jefferson was a physically strong man whose courage was well known. He told Tom that it is the strong in body who are both strong and free in mind. Therefore, along with his studies, Tom was taught to love the outdoors. The young boy was instructed to set aside four hours a day for physical exercise. He walked through the countryside, rode a horse, and hunted and fished in the Southwest Mountains, enjoying his childhood.

When the Jefferson family returned to Shadwell, Tom, then about nine years old, began a second phase in his education. He was enrolled at a school between Shadwell and Tuckahoe taught by the Reverend William Douglas. It was a Latin school, where Jefferson learned the classical languages of Latin and Greek. Douglas also introduced Tom to French. Because the school was far from home, Tom boarded there and visited his home every three or four months. Jefferson loved to learn and later said that there was nothing more "sublime" than reading literature in their original languages.

Tom was not completely happy at Douglas's school. He felt that the clergyman was only a "superficial Latinist" and was even worse in teaching Greek.

However, he did develop a talent on his own. During the six years he attended Douglas's school, Jefferson started to teach himself how to play the fiddle. He practiced three hours a day and gradually became an accomplished violinist.

Tragedy deeply affected Thomas Jefferson's life in 1757, when he was fourteen years old. His father died suddenly, leaving Tom with the responsibility for seven younger siblings. It was a difficult time for him, as he recalled years later:

> When I recollect that at fourteen years of age, the whole care and direction of my self was thrown on my self entirely, without a relation or friend qualified to advise and guide me, and recollect the various sorts of bad company with which I associated from time to time, I am astonished that I did not turn off with some of them, and become as worthless to society as they were…

Yet, it was his continued interest in education that protected him.

Jefferson eventually inherited 5,000 acres from his father's estate. The income from this land supported him while he continued to develop his knowledge. Thomas always felt there were two things his father left him that were most valuable. One was his father's library of forty books, a real treasure in those days. The other was Peter's deathbed wish that Thomas would pursue a classical education. Thomas Jefferson always remembered his father with great love and respect, admiring him for his kindness, his physical strength and his love of learning.

After his father's death, Tom's guardians sent him to a new Latin school established in the parish of Fredericksville at Hanover. It was run by the Reverend James Maury, who became like a second father to Jefferson. Reverend Maury was a demanding teacher but one who had a great intellect and a gift for teaching. Jefferson boarded there for two years and found it to be one of the most enjoyable times of his life. Reverend Maury continued to teach him Latin, Greek, and French, but now Jefferson felt he was in a "real" Latin school. He spent much of his time in Maury's four-hundred-volume library, pouring over its books.

In addition to the classical languages, Jefferson began to read some English literature, geography, history, and math. He studied English composition and learned how to speak in clear and persuasive grammar, although this shy young man always shunned public speaking. Maury took his students on field trips through the Virginia countryside and taught them zoology, geology, physics, and chemistry.

Jefferson's classmates realized that he was a serious student. He would sit under an oak tree and study Latin and Greek while the other students played. Jefferson studied the next day's lesson before he joined his friends. Maury taught him some of the same lessons as his father had—especially the value of self-discipline and patience.

During the two years at Maury's school, Jefferson began a practice that would continue for the next fifteen years, throughout his entire school experience. He started to keep a literary commonplace book. In it, Jefferson wrote down selected

135

April. 16.th 1768.

Present as before mention'd.

The Report of John Camm & Emmanuel Jones.

In obedience to the order of the President & Masters pass'd yesterday, we waited upon John Carnshaw Esq.r and were by his favour permitted to examine the certain Books in his possession, by which it appears to us that the Sum of three hundred and thirty five pounds nineteen shillings and six pence current money has been received for Duties on Tobacco en-ter'd in the upper district of James River from October 15.th 1763 to September 28.th 1764. and the Sum of one hundred and sixty five pounds nine shillings and two pence sterling for Duties on Tobacco entr'd in the said district from September 28.th 1764 to May 29.th 1765. and it also appears to us that no pay-ment has been made to the College on account of either of the above Sums. For the particulars from whence the above conclusions are drawn we refer to the Schedule in the 137 & 138th Pages in this Book.

Resol: that Mr. Blair be desir'd to examine the said

The College of William and Mary was founded in 1693. To support the school and to pay for the construction of its first building, the Virginia House of Burgesses enacted a special "importation tax" upon "skins and furrs" as well as a new tobacco tax. Faculty salaries were paid from this tax. Good tobacco crops meant higher salaries, while failed years resulted in almost no wages. (Today, this would be similar to having one's salary pegged to the rise and fall of the stock market.) This tobacco tax, its enforcement and collection, remained a point of contention between Virginia tobacco planters and the college until the American Revolution. In the above document, the president of William and Mary ordered that the "books" of a James River tobacco planter be audited for the period October 15, 1763, to September 28, 1764, because it "appears to us that no payment has been made to the College."

Bursar's Books, College of William and Mary, 1763–64

When Jefferson attended William and Mary from 1760 to 1762, the enrollment was slightly more than one hundred students. (Slaves who were servants to the wealthier boys were not counted.) Less than a dozen Native Americans, or Indians, were enrolled in a special school with the aim of converting them to Christianity and to amalgamate them into "white society." The "college is at present in a very peaceable & thriving Way, & has now more Scholars in it, than it has ever had from its Foundation," President William Stith wrote to the Bishop of London in 1753.

Two years later, the Virginia tobacco crop failed. To cope with the desperate situation, the colonial legislature passed a law that for the next ten months—until the harvesting of the 1756 crop—all debts legally payable in tobacco could be paid in paper money at a rate fixed by law. Fortunately, 1756 and 1757 yielded outstanding tobacco crops. Nevertheless, the paper money law was reenacted. The William and Mary faculty considered the legislature's act as an attack upon them and the college, both dependent upon the price of tobacco and both opposed to being paid in paper money. In 1755 and 1756, faculty members, along with a quarter of Virginia's total Anglican clergy (whose salaries also were dependent upon the price of tobacco), protested to the Bishop of London about being paid in paper money rather than from the fees raised through the tobacco tax. But their protests were to no avail.

The above document details faculty salaries for 1763–64. The column on the right is the sums due in pound sterling. The column on the left is the sum actually paid in the depreciated local currency.

passages from the books he was reading. He summarized what he read and picked out what he felt were the key ideas and most inspiring thoughts. The earliest portions are from the writings of Horace, Virgil, and Ovid, who Jefferson studied while at Maury's school. Later, when he attended college, Jefferson continued to write in his commonplace book, adding selections from such Greek writers as Homer, Euripides, and Herodotus.

Jefferson eventually published the *Literary Commonplace Book* in the 1780s. It was a small book, four by six inches, with one hundred and twenty-three pages. The book was divided into sections of prose, classical poetry, English poetry, English dramatic verse, and miscellaneous poetry.

After two years at Maury's Latin school, Jefferson was ready to begin a new phase of his formal education. In March 1760, just before his seventeenth birthday, Jefferson left Shadwell for the one hundred and twenty-eight mile trip to Williamsburg, Virginia. He wanted to fulfill his father's dream—and secure his own future—by enrolling in the College of William and Mary. Thomas Jefferson also understood that in Williamsburg he would make contact with influential people who could further his ambitions.

Williamsburg was the largest town Thomas Jefferson had ever seen. It was the capital of the Virginia colony, the seat of political life, and the social and cultural heart of all the southern colonies. The mile-long Duke of Gloucester Street was the heart of the town with the college at one end and the capitol building at the other. When Jefferson enrolled in college, the town had about two hundred one-story houses with many large mansions. The population was normally between one thousand and fifteen hundred, but when the General Court and House of Burgesses were in session in the spring and fall, the population doubled. It was an exciting place to study for a young man arriving from the Virginia frontier. Here, at the seat of the provincial government, Jefferson witnessed history in the making and politics in practice.

The oldest higher education institution in the South, the College of William and Mary had been chartered in 1693 by King William III and Queen Mary II. From its beginning, the school was intended to be both a seminary for Anglican clergy and a college for the sons of the wealthy Virginia planters. In 1760, the college had six professors, including one who taught in the Indian School, which was devoted to the conversion and teaching of Native Americans. There was a struggle going on at the time of Jefferson's attendance between those who wanted the college to be secular and those who felt its first priority should be religious.

Jefferson enrolled in the Philosophy School, much like a liberal arts school today, and was eager to study the classics and mathematics. There he met William Small, one of the three men in Williamsburg who would have a powerful influence on his life. Young Jefferson was taught solely by Small, who had arrived in Williamsburg shortly before Jefferson. He was the only non-clergyman on the faculty. Small had been educated at Aberdeen, Scotland, and had a brilliant mind. He was well trained in science, then called natural philosophy, and taught a variety of other subjects.

Soon, Jefferson was learning logic, physics, ethics, philosophy, history, and rhetoric. Professor Small appreciated Jefferson's eagerness to learn, and the two became close friends. It was Small who introduced Thomas Jefferson to the ideas of the Enlightenment, a movement that had spread across Europe and into the colonies. This philosophy rejected many traditional ideas about religion and politics and encouraged people to use reason alone for guidance. Later in his life, Jefferson credited William Small as determining the direction of his life.

Jefferson continued to consume books. He read Montesquieu, Voltaire, and Rousseau in French, Cicero in Latin, and English authors like Shakespeare, Chaucer, and Milton. The scope of his reading was broad and included the science of Isaac Newton, which challenged many popular scientific theories. He began to teach himself Spanish and even Anglo-Saxon so that he could understand the roots of English common law.

Professor Small introduced Jefferson to the second man who would alter his life, George Wythe, the most noted lawyer of his generation in Virginia. Wythe and his wife had no children, and so they treated Tom as if he were their son. Jefferson thoroughly enjoyed his friendship with Wythe and considered him his "faithful and beloved mentor." They were to remain friends for many years. Wythe would one day sign the Declaration of Independence, which was written by Thomas Jefferson.

Jefferson was next introduced to Governor Francis Fauquier, an important figure in Virginia society and the third man to make a lasting impression on him. The three older men and student Thomas Jefferson became fast friends and met together regularly. The four often had dinner at the Governor's Palace near the college. Jefferson loved these informal dinners and felt that he heard more interesting and meaningful conversation there than at any time in his life. Fauquier was also a good musician and often asked Jefferson to play the violin in quartets that he arranged.

At the same time that Jefferson was enjoying the company of these established leaders of Virginia, he was also a typical college student. He was a recognized member of a close-knit social group made up of the children of the great families of Virginia. Jefferson and some of his teenage friends from Maury's Latin school, who were also attending William and Mary, formed a secret club. They called it the Flat Hat Club, and spoke what they dubbed "pig Latin." They met in the Apollo Room of the Raleigh Tavern, just up Duke of Gloucester Street from the House of Burgesses. These friends would have a major influence on Jefferson's career.

Jefferson graduated from the College of William and Mary in two years and entered the final phase of his formal education. In 1762, he decided to study law under George Wythe. He became a part of a group of young men also studying with this famous lawyer which included John Marshall, later the fourth chief justice of the U.S. Supreme Court; James Monroe, one day to become the fifth president of the United States; and Henry Clay, secretary of state under John Quincy Adams.

**"Desperate Debts," Bursar's Books,
College of William and Mary, 1764–68**

In the 1760s the College of William and Mary was close to bankruptcy. Most of the sums due the college just did not come in. Tobacco-duty frauds continued unabated. For almost twenty years, the college had not received one penny of the revenue due it on imported skins and furs. This "desperate debts" page listed money overdue the college. Interest charges were regularly added. Benjamin Harrison, the Revolutionary statesman and governor of Virginia, is among those listed on this page as owing the school money in 1764–65. Harrison, who served in the House of Burgesses (1749–75), also owned one of the largest estates in Virginia. The sums due were from the unpaid tobacco tax. Likewise, John Carter, another large Virginia landholder, is listed as delinquent in paying the tobacco tax to William and Mary for 1764–67.

Norborne Berkeley, Baron de Botetourt (c. 1718–1770)

Thomas Jefferson considered his academic studies at William and Mary to be decidedly useful. Without a doubt, this was because of William Small. The other three or four faculty members were dullards.

In 1785, twenty-three years after leaving William and Mary, Jefferson wrote a rousing testimonial to the teaching that he had received:

> But why send an American youth to Europe for education? What are the objects of an [sic] useful American education? Classical knowledge, modern languages, chiefly French, Spanish, and Italian; Mathematics, Natural philosophy, Natural history, Civil history, and Ethics. In Natural Philosophy, I mean to include Chemistry and Agriculture, and in Natural history, to include Botany, as well as the other branches of those departments. It is true that the habit of speaking the modern languages cannot be so well acquired in America; but every other article can be as well acquired at William and Mary college as at any place in Europe.

Actually, Jefferson was describing the major academic changes that had occurred at William and Mary after he left the school. One person who stands out for having had a profound effect upon raising standards was Norborne Berkeley, Baron de Botetourt.

Lord Botetourt was appointed governor of Virginia in 1768. He was related to the prominent Berkeley family of Virginia and London. Instead of appointing a deputy to perform his duties, Botetourt went out to the colony in person, becoming the first royal governor in almost seventy-five years to take up permanent residence in Virginia. He brought over with him a resplendent coach and a team of cream-white Hanoverian horses. Botetourt promptly summoned the Virginia General Assembly. Dressed in a red coat, decorated with gold braiding, he was driven to the Capitol in his glittering coach drawn by his horses in their silver mounted harnesses—the whole an imitation of King George III opening the British Parliament. He delivered his address as if reading it from the royal throne. Some present said he even imitated the mannerisms of the monarch. But the burgesses were not awed by this pomp and circumstance. When they reasserted their rights not to be transported overseas to be tried by English juries, Botetourt rebuked them for their boldness and dissolved them as a body. Most of the burgesses reassembled at a local tavern. They unanimously adopted a resolution offered by George Washington that they would neither import nor buy any article that was subject to a parliamentary tax. This resolution began a path to the American Revolution.

Botetourt died in 1770, two years after his arrival in Virginia. During this brief period, he took an active role in the college as rector of the William and Mary Board of Visitors. Exacerbated by student vandalism and the continued insolvency of the school, Botetourt set about to improve both its physical and academic fabric.

His intervention in the academic life of William and Mary was immediate. To encourage scholarship, the governor offered two gold medals annually, one for classical learning and the other for achievement in natural philosophy [science]. These medals were to be awarded after a vigorous and thorough competition. These honors were given to students enrolled in the college for at least one year and who also demonstrated "moral conduct as members of society" as well as academic merit. The Botetourt Medals were the first medals presented by an academic institution in America. The College of William and Mary still awards the Lord Botetourt Medal on Commencement Day to the graduating senior who ranks first academically.

Botetourt's interest in the education at William and Mary was a real one. He took part in student's oral examinations. Until Botetourt, and in the almost eighty years since the college had received its royal charter, the college had not conferred one bachelor's degree. Botetourt had the scientific apparatus, which had been in storage since William Small departed, dusted off and used again. Encouraged by him, the F.H.C., a scholastic society which when Jefferson had been a student had by his own account "no useful object," suddenly took on the preparation of a highly sophisticated reading list and began plans for the purchase of a considerable library.

After Botetourt's death in 1770, a marble statue was erected in his honor. It stands in the quadrangle of the College of William and Mary.

Under Wythe's direction, Jefferson studied the writings of English jurists Sir William Blackstone and Edward Coke. Jefferson also studied English law as well as Virginia colonial law.

Thomas Jefferson continued to show the self-discipline that had helped him become such a good student. He awoke each morning at five, read ethics, religion, and natural law until eight, and then studied law until lunch. In the afternoon he returned to his study of law and then would visit friends. In late afternoon he would read history and at night, for relaxation, read literature. Jefferson studied approximately fifteen hours a day. In addition to that heavy schedule, Jefferson continued to set aside two hours every day for walking.

For the next five years, from 1762 to 1767, Jefferson studied under George Wythe. Whenever the General Court was in session and Wythe was in Williamsburg, Jefferson went to his home to read in his excellent library. Jefferson was given cases to research and prepare for Wythe and then went with him to the General Court in Williamsburg. When Wythe traveled to county courts around Virginia, Jefferson often went with him. During the latter part of his association with Wythe, Jefferson began to argue cases by himself in the courts. He was practically Wythe's law partner. In April of 1767, when Jefferson was twenty-four, he was admitted to the Virginia bar. He would practice law until 1774, when the courts were closed by unrest in the colonies.

Jefferson's formal education came to an end when he was twenty-four, but he continued to expand his knowledge and skills throughout his life. After he became a successful lawyer, he returned to Shadwell and began to build a new house on his estate. He leveled the top of a mountain and began to build on the summit. He named his new home Monticello ("small mountain"). Building on a height was unknown in the colonies, but it was an idea Jefferson had learned from books he had

Front and back views of copper striking of the Botetourt Medal, done as a proof, c. 1772

read on architecture. He was especially influenced by the sixteenth-century Italian, Andrea Palladio, whose text *Four Books of Architecture* taught Jefferson that there were laws of architecture, just as there were laws of mathematics and physical laws.

When he was twenty-eight, Jefferson met and married Martha Wayles Skelton, the twenty-three year old widow of a former classmate from William and Mary; she had a young son from her previous marriage. They were married on January 1, 1772, at The Forest, an estate owned by Martha's wealthy lawyer father. They settled at an incomplete Monticello. The Jeffersons had a happy marriage, which produced six children before Martha died after childbirth on September 6, 1782. Jefferson mourned his wife deeply and never remarried.

Thomas Jefferson's political career began when he was only twenty-six. He was first elected to the House of Burgesses in 1769, representing Albemarle County. He would serve in the House of Burgesses until he became a member of the Continental Congress in 1775. Thomas Jefferson was the principal author of the Declaration of Independence in 1776. This famous document, written without reference to a single book, showed the brilliance of his mind and the depth of his knowledge.

Jefferson was governor of Virginia from 1779 until 1781, during the American Revolution. He was elected to Congress in 1783 and served until 1785. He sailed for Europe in 1785 as the minister to France for the new United States of America and remained there until 1789. After his return to America, he became the first secretary of state under George Washington, a position he held from 1790 to 1793. Jefferson was elected vice president under John Adams and served in that position from 1797 until 1801.

In 1801, Jefferson became the third president of the United States, in an election decided by the House of Representatives when the electoral vote ended in a tie between Jefferson and Aaron Burr. He was elected to a second term in 1804. While president, Thomas Jefferson oversaw the Louisiana Purchase, which greatly increased the size of the United States, and authorized the Lewis and Clark expedition.

Thomas Jefferson retired from politics in 1809, at the end of his second term as president, and returned to his beloved Monticello. Home in Virginia, Jefferson founded the University of Virginia at Charlottesville in 1825, designing its buildings and managing its construction.

Late in his life, Jefferson sold his collection of 6,487 books for $23,950 to the U.S. government to replace a library that had been destroyed by British troops when they burned Washington, D.C., during the war of 1812. The money helped Jefferson pay an enormous debt he had because of a bad loan to a friend and debts inherited from his father-in-law. Jefferson's extensive collection had to be carried to Washington in eleven wagons, and became the basis for the developing Library of Congress. However, it was not long before his love for books led Jefferson to purchase new volumes and begin another library at Monticello.

In 1826, as Jefferson passed his eighty-third birthday, he became increasingly ill. His good friend and correspondent, former president John Adams, was also in very poor health. The two had both signed the Declaration of Independence in 1776 and were hoping to live until its fiftieth anniversary on July 4. As the fourth approached, Jefferson passed in and out of consciousness. He kept asking, "Is it the fourth yet?" Finally, in the early hours of July 4, 1826, Jefferson died, just a few hours before John Adams.

Thomas Jefferson was a lifelong student. He never stopped learning and never stopped being optimistic about what education could do. He believed that each new generation would build upon the knowledge of the past and work toward the well-being of human beings. For him, education was essential to a good life and to a beneficial existence. "Education," he once wrote, "engrafts a new man on the native stock, and improves what in his nature was vicious and perverse into qualities of virtue and social worth."

The value of education instilled in him by his father served him well. On the simple stone over his grave in the family burial ground at Monticello, he is described as he wished to be remembered, not as the holder of great offices, but as the author of the Declaration of Independence, and the Virginia statute for religious freedom, and the father of the University of Virginia.

—Bill Thompson

James Madison
C h a p t e r   F o u r

During March 1751, James and Nellie Madison traveled for three days over the rough dirt roads of colonial Virginia. They were on the way to Nellie's parents' home on the Rappahannock River, just across from the tidewater town of Port Royal. The couple was fifty miles away from their own home, but Nellie wanted to be with her mother when she gave birth to her first child.

At midnight on March 16, 1751, the baby arrived. It was a boy, whom the couple named James after his father. As Nellie held her son for the first time, she had no idea what the future held in store. Virginia was still a colony of Great Britain, and the United States did not yet exist. Yet this infant would one day be a key figure among the men who formed the government of the United States, as well as the country's fourth president.

James Madison Jr. was born into a prosperous family. Ambrose Madison, the grandfather of baby James, had settled in Orange Country on five thousand acres in 1729. With his wife, Frances, and three children, he developed an estate, which he called Mount Pleasant. (It would later be renamed Montpelier.)

Ambrose died in 1731, leaving his thirty-one-year-old widow to manage the tobacco estate herself. With her twenty-nine slaves, Frances became a successful Virginia planter, selling her tobacco crop in England. She was interested in developing the education of her children and made sure that her contacts in London sent her books and the *Spectator,* the leading magazine of the day. Her son James, educated as a child by Frances, began to help on the estate when he was only nine years old.

James Madison Sr. eventually inherited Montpelier and continued developing it. Soon, Montpelier was the largest plantation in the county, with more than one hundred slaves. When James was twenty-six years old, he married seventeen-year-old Nellie Conway. It was just a little more than eighteen months later that the couple welcomed their first child, James Jr. A few weeks later, they returned to Montpelier and continued their life there, along with James' mother, Frances. James and Nellie would have eleven more children, but only seven of the Madison children lived to maturity.

Grandmother Frances was James Jr.'s first teacher. There were no public

Princeton University (The College of New Jersey)

Princeton University, founded as the College of New Jersey in 1746, is the fourth-oldest institution of higher education in the United States. At the time, no college existed between Yale in New Haven, Connecticut, and the College of William and Mary in Williamsburg, Virginia. Princeton's John Witherspoon was the only college president to sign the Declaration of Independence (1776). It was in Princeton's Nassau Hall in 1783 that General George Washington received the formal thanks of the Continental Congress for his conduct of the American Revolution. Nine of the fifty-five members of the Constitutional Convention (1787) were Princeton graduates—more than from any other college.

Like its predecessors—Harvard, William and Mary, and Yale—Princeton was established by a religious denomination. It came into being because of the Great Awakening, that famous religious revival during the second quarter of the eighteenth century. Emphasizing the need of a personal religious experience, revivalists like Gilbert Tennent, his father and brother, and George Whitefield attracted multitudes of adherents by their fiery exhortations to sinners to repent. In the Presbyterian Church, these believers were known as New Lights (as opposed to the Old Sides, who preferred a more conservative religious doctrine). It was the New Light group that was instrumental in the founding of Princeton to educate ministers for their rapidly increasing churches. In 1748, Jonathan Belcher, the colonial governor of New Jersey, gave the new school his personal library of four hundred and seventy-four volumes, instantly making the college library one of the largest in the colonies.

Serious education came into young James Madison's life when his father sent him to the small local school of Edinburgh-trained Donald Robertson. Years later, when he was president of the United States, Madison wrote that Robertson was "a man of great learning, and an eminent teacher." Robertson instilled in Madison a love for learning. Madison's next tutor was Thomas Martin, a Presbyterian minister who had graduated from the College of New Jersey at Princeton in 1762. Martin served as a "family teacher" as he taught James, his three brothers and sister, and some neighbors children as well. Martin directed Madison to Princeton. Young Madison appreciated the opportunity to travel nearly three hundred miles from his native Virginia. And so, in 1769, eighteen-year-old James Madison set off to Princeton accompanied by Thomas Martin, Martin's brother, and Sawney, a Madison family slave and servant.

Student life at Princeton in the early 1770s was dominated by routine. There were about eighty students. Nassau Hall, which opened in 1756, contained the classrooms, a kitchen and dining area, and the student living quarters. Madison's classmate Philip Vickers Fithian, recorded the following schedule:

5-5:30 A.M. Dressing period. "The Bell rings at five, after which there is an Intermission of half an hour, that everyone may have time to dress, at the end of which it rings again, and Prayers begin; And lest any should plead that he did not hear the Bell, the Servant who rings goes to every Door and beats till he wakens the Boys."

5:30 Morning Prayers. "After Morning Prayers, we can, now in the winter, study by candle Light every Morning."

8:00 Breakfast. "From eight to nine is time of our own, to play, or exercise."

9:00-1:00 Recitation.

1:00 Dinner. "We all dine in the same Room, at three tables. After dinner till three we have Liberty to go out at Pleasure."

3:00-5:00 Study.

5:00 Evening Prayers

7:00 Supper.

9:00 "At nine the Bell rings for Study; And a Tutor goes through College, to see that every Student is in his own Room; if he finds that any are absent, or more in any Room than belongs there, he notes them down, and the day following calls them to an Account. After nine any may go to bed, but to go before is reproachful."

John Witherspoon, president of the College of New Jersey, 1768–94

James Madison's arrival at Princeton coincided with the arrival of John Witherspoon as the new college president. Witherspoon's years at Princeton are considered one of the must illustrious administrations in the college's history. Witherspoon, a descendant of John Knox and the choice of the New Lights, held views that were welcome to those of the Old Side. The traditional classical and religious education was maintained but Witherspoon introduced into the curriculum the study of eighteenth-century philosophy, French, modern history, and oratory. He insisted upon a mastery of the English language. Witherspoon altered the college's original mission. It was his conviction that an education should fit a man for public usefulness, not only for the pulpit. Book learning for its own sake did not appeal to him. From 1768 to 1776, the College of New Jersey increased its student body, the faculty, and the college endowment. From the favorable comments of Madison and others who studied at Princeton before the American Revolution, it seems that life at the college was progressive and stimulating.

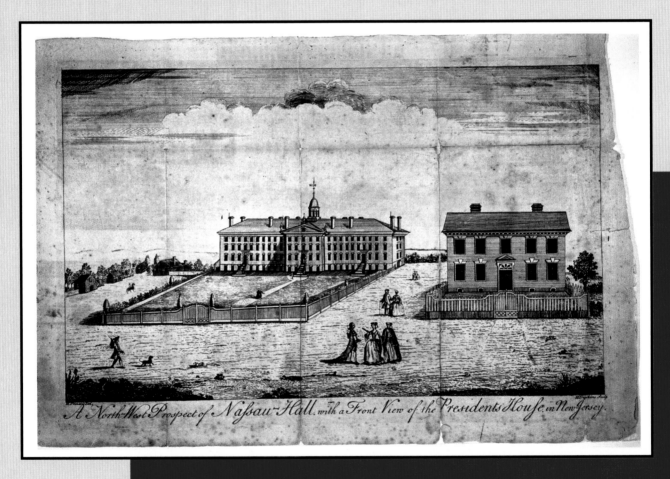

A North-West Prospect of Nassau-Hall, with a Front View of the Presidents House in New Jersey.

Copper Engraving of Princeton's Nassau Hall and the President's House, 1764, by Henry Dawkins.
Henry Dawkins, a Philadelphia artist, copied this 1764 engraving of Nassau Hall and the president's house at Princeton from a drawing by William Tennant, class of 1758. James Madison lived in Nassau Hall for three years, 1769–72.
Witherspoon is credited with first applying the word *campus* (Latin for "field") to the college setting rather than calling it a yard, as was usual then. His description stuck, and gradually the word campus was adopted by universities throughout the nation.

schools in Virginia at this time, so most children received their educations at home. Frances taught her grandson reading, writing, and arithmetic, and encouraged him to read the *Spectator* before he was in his teens. He remembered the benefits he received from the magazine all his life. "It was good," James wrote to a young nephew years later, "for stirring in your mind a desire for improvement, a taste for learning and a lively sense of the duties, the virtues and the proprieties of life."

Jemmy, as young James was called, was a typical Virginia boy and loved taking long walks, horseback riding, and hunting and fishing with his many cousins who lived nearby. Yet Jemmy's first love was books and study. He enjoyed reading in his father's library more than playing outdoors.

When Jemmy was still young, the Madison family moved into a new brick mansion just a half mile away. This estate would be his home for the rest of his life.

For Jemmy, one of the most important rooms in the new home was the library. He read any book he could understand. Many of the books were religious and included *The Gospel Mystery of Sanctification, Warning to a Careless World*, and *The Nature of Sin*. These books expanded Jemmy's mind and gave him an interest in the the study of divinity. However, the library also contained books such as *The Motion of Fluids* and *The Dictionary of Arts and Sciences*, which described the latest scientific studies and discoveries. Jemmy read from those as well, and during his childhood developed an interest in science.

When Jemmy was ten, his Grandmother Frances died. To continue his education, Jemmy was sent to a boarding school run by Donald Robertson. Robertson had been educated at Aberdeen and Edinburgh in Scotland and had started his school along the Mattapony River just four years before eleven-year-old Jemmy arrived to join some of his cousins already attending the school.

It was while Madison studied with Robertson that he came alive intellectually. When, as an old man, Madison looked back over his life, he recalled the education he received at Robertson's school: "All that I have been in life I owe largely to that man." He studied English and mathematics during his first year, beginning his studies with a book called *Rudiments*. After this Jamie—as Robertson called the young man—went on to study Latin and Greek. He read Latin writings by the Roman poets Virgil, Horace, and Ovid as well as the Roman historians Cornelius Nepos and Sallust. In his final year, Madison concentrated on Greek and read many Greek classics, including the biographer Plutarch, the philosopher Plato, and the historian Herodotus.

Madison also studied Spanish and French. Unfortunately, in learning these languages he accidentally picked up Robertson's strong Scottish accent. This would make his conversation in the languages almost impossible to understand, as he would find out later in college. Madison also studied geography, history, and a variety of literature. Robertson's large library contained writings by the French essayist Montaigne and the political philosopher Montesquieu as well as the English philosopher John Locke. Madison read these and began developing his interest in the workings of government.

Before Madison arrived at Robertson's boarding school, he had begun a commonplace book like many other young men of his day. It is dated 1759, when Madison was only eight years old, but it probably contains things he copied at Robertson's school and possibly during his college years. It is a twenty-four-page notebook in which he copied some of the poems he was reading as well as articles from the *Spectator* and his own thoughts about authors he was reading. It shows clearly his ability to understand ideas and summarize them well. He was interested in the nature of human beings and the theories of government.

Another notebook that Madison filled out, dated 1766, was called "Notes on a Brief System of Logic." It has one hundred and twenty-two pages, and in them Madison included summaries of lectures given by his teacher and notes taken during class. There are references to writers such as Socrates and Euclid. At the end of the notebook are drawings and astronomical charts, including "The Solar System from Copernicus," a sixteenth-century Polish astronomer. Because some of the thinking is so mature, some scholars surmise that many of the notes might have been done when he was in college several years later.

Madison graduated from Donald Robertson's school on September 9, 1767, and returned to Montpelier for the next phase of his education. Reverend Thomas Martin had become rector at the Brick Church, not far from Montpelier. He lived at the Madison home; in return, he acted as tutor for the family. With Martin's guidance, Madison's understanding of Greek and Latin continued to deepen over the next two years.

The greatest influence Thomas Martin had on young Madison's life, however, was to direct him toward the College of New Jersey, later to be called Princeton University. Martin had graduated from that school just five years before coming to Montpelier and often spoke about its advantages. Thomas's brother, Alexander, also a recent graduate of the College of New Jersey, often visited Thomas Martin at Montpelier, and he too raved about the college.

Both brothers, though active churchmen, were opposed to the power of the Episcopal Church in Virginia. They disapproved of the establishment of a state-supported church that was financed through government taxes, which was the case in the Virginia Colony. Because William and Mary College in Williamsburg had been founded by the Episcopal Church and was closely connected to the political leaders of Virginia, they did not speak favorably of it. The College of New Jersey had been created by "New Side" Presbyterians, who stressed evangelism and religious freedom. Madison, who had witnessed the oppression of Baptists by the Episcopal Church in Virginia, appreciated a Presbyterian college that did not support the power of the clergy. When Madison was eighteen years old, he decided to go to the College of New Jersey.

Madison arrived in Princeton during the spring of 1769. The College of New Jersey had been founded in 1746 and so was only twenty-three years old when Madison arrived. Yet, it was probably the most diverse of the five colleges in America, with students coming from each of the colonies. When Madison attended

These Board of Trustees minutes were written while James Madison was a student at Princeton, 1769–71.

The page on the left focuses on financial problems. President John Witherspoon set the college on a sound financial basis, often raising funds by traveling through the colonies to recruit students. Although Princeton punished students who engaged in games of chance, officials saw no contradiction in holding a lottery for the benefit of the college. For example, in 1772 Delaware held a lottery for the "College of New Jersey, the Presbyterian Congregation of Princetown [Princeton], and the United Presbyterian Congregations of New Castle in Christiana Bridge." The proceeds to these three groups constituted fifteen percent of the prize money.

On the right page, dated September 26, 1770, the Board of Trustees conferred honorary doctorates of divinity on five ministers. The following day, September 27, the Board dealt with raising money in other colonies for support of the college. Noteworthy here is the mention of Richard Stockton, class of 1748. In 1766 Stockton, as a trustee of the college, was asked by the board to offer the college presidency to John Witherspoon, then living near Glasgow, Scotland. Stockton, a future signer of the Declaration of Independence, was received in London by King George III. He was given the freedom of the city of Edinburgh at a public dinner. However, Stockton could not convince Mrs. Witherspoon to move from Glasgow to Princeton. Undaunted, Stockton wrote to his wife: "I have engaged all the eminent clergymen in Edinburgh and Glasgow to attack her in her intrenchments and they are determined to take her by storm, if nothing else will do." Finally, after prolonged negotiations, Mrs. Witherspoon yielded and the Stockton mission was successful.

Friday Sept. 28 at 8 O'Clock A.M.

Then met according to Adjournment & present as Yesterday —

Mr. Sym who was heretofore appointed the College Librarian, having removed some time ago from hence, and it being now represented that sufficient care is not taken of the Books for want of a properly established Librarian who may be answerable for all lost & damaged Books — To remedy this inconvenience the Trustees now thought fit to appoint Mr. William Houston to be the College Librarian & Keeper of the Philosophical Apparatus: who shall immediately cause all the Books to be collected together & properly arranged, and provide himself with a proper Book in which he shall enter a very exact Catalogue of all the Books belonging to the Library, & shall keep exact & punctual Entries in the same of all the Books that may be taken out & returned by the Students who shall be answerable to him for all Books lost or damaged by them respectively — The Librarian shall be at liberty to appoint a Deputy under him for whose Conduct he shall himself be responsible to this Board — He shall never allow the Library to be opened for any Student to enter in, or any Strangers be admitted but in his or his Deputy's presence — He shall also by himself or Deputy be obliged to give a regular Attendance twice in every Week for the space of one hour for delivering out Books to the Students who shall be allowed but one Book at a time, and the said Librarian shall keep in best and most exact Order all the Instruments for the Philosophical Experiments now belonging or that shall hereafter belong to the College in some proper Room to be set apart for that purpose by the President, nor shall he ever suffer any of them to be viewed or handled but in his or his Deputy's presence, unless by any one of the Officers of the College; or when they may be made use of by them in the Instruction of their Pupils — And in Order to satisfy the said Librarian for his services in keeping the Library and Apparatus It is Ordered that the Steward do charge in the Quarterly Bills eighteen pence for Quarter in every Student or resident Graduate belonging to this College, & that he pay the same unto the said Librarian or his Order — And the President is desired, in conjunction with the Librarian to draw up a set of Rules and Regulations for the better management of the Library &c. to be laid before the Trustees at their next Meeting, but which on publication shall be immediately binding on all the Students & Residents of the College —

The Honble William Smith of New York one of the Members of this Board being deceased, the Board proceeded to the Choice of a Trustee in his room when the

When James Madison was a student at Princeton, the library contained about two thousand books. This total included the five hundred or so volumes that John Witherspoon brought with him from Scotland when he assumed the college presidency in 1768. Witherspoon consistently ordered more books, with special emphasis on works in English. The above page from the Board of Trustees minutes (left) deals with the appointment of a new librarian. Among his other tasks, the librarian was given the responsibility of cataloging the books and maintaining better management of the library.

the College of New Jersey, only nineteen of the eighty-four students attending were from New Jersey. In his graduating class, only one of the twelve graduates was from New Jersey. That was a contrast to other colonial colleges, where the student bodies were made up mostly of men from the colonies in which the schools were located.

The president of the college in 1769 was a Presbyterian clergyman, Dr. John Witherspoon, who had come from Scotland the year before. He was considered a man of great learning who had much personal charm. In Scotland, Witherspoon had been exposed to the Enlightenment, a movement that rejected traditional social, religious, and political ideas. Witherspoon brought their books and ideas to Princeton. Witherspoon was conservative in his theology but liberal in his politics. He had a strong influence on Madison and other students of the college at a time when the colonies were being stirred by ideas of freedom from Great Britain. The College of New Jersey graduated more signers of the Declaration of Independence than any of the other colonial colleges.

Madison was tested when he entered the College of New Jersey and, because of his excellent early education, was able to enroll as a sophomore. Along with another student, he received permission to accelerate his studies so he could finish the remaining three years in two and graduate in 1771. In order to complete the accelerated schedule, Madison went for weeks with only five hours of sleep a night. He became thoroughly engrossed in his studies.

School began in November and continued for twenty-one weeks until April. After a five-week break, school resumed in May and went for another twenty-one weeks until September. Madison studied a variety of subjects. He continued to develop his knowledge of the classics, and in his first year studied astronomy, geography, algebra, rhetoric, French, and debating. Later he took mathematics and natural philosophy (physics and astronomy). Witherspoon himself taught courses in history and moral philosophy to Madison when he was a senior.

Life was full for Madison; he not only excelled in his studies but made many friends. The students had classes in Nassau Hall and also lived there together, three men to a room. One of Madison's friends was a college tutor, Samuel Stanhope Smith, who eventually succeeded Witherspoon as president of the College of New Jersey. Another friend was William Bradford, who studied divinity while in Princeton and later became a lawyer.

Right after entering college, Madison joined the newly formed American Whig Society. This was a literary organization in which friendships were developed as literature and essays about the issues of the time were read, discussed, and debated. The private debates, on such issues as freedom from British rule, whetted Madison's appetite for government.

In 1770, another literary society was formed, the Cliosophic Society, which began a "paper war" with the Whigs; one of its leaders was Aaron Burr. The public debates between the two societies often became more exciting than class work. Leaders of both societies would write satires that ridiculed the other.

Madison was one author for the Whigs, along with Philip Freneau and Henry Brackenridge, who were both excellent poets.

While not the equal of Freneau and Brackenridge in poetry, Madison wrote one satire that mocked Moses Allen, the founder of the Cliosophics. He called him "Great Allen" and assigned him a place in "Pluto's realm" (hell). Some of Madison's satires were too vulgar to be printed and were later repressed by his friends and biographers. Because Madison's humorous side was often unrecorded, later generations often thought of him as formal and stuffy. Yet the satires show a casual side of Madison. It was all in good fun, though. Moses Allen would become a pastor and visit Madison at Montpelier.

It was in Princeton that Madison realized how poorly he had learned French. President Witherspoon entertained a French diplomat as a guest of the college. Hearing that the young student had learned French fluently in Virginia, Witherspoon asked Madison to interpret for him. However, Madison spoke with such a Scottish burr that the Frenchman could not understand one word he said. This episode became one of Madison's favorite dinner stories for the remainder of his life.

The political situation in the American colonies greatly affected the College of New Jersey during Madison's years there. During the 1760s, the colonies were arguing with the British Parliament over the right of England to tax the colonies without their consent. The Townshend Acts of 1767 placed duties on many American imports. Boston merchants decided not to import goods from England, and many American cities, including New York and Philadelphia, joined the boycott.

In the summer of 1770, when Madison was in his second year at the College of New Jersey, the students learned of a letter written by the merchants of New York to the merchants of Philadelphia. The letter asked the Philadelphia merchants to join them in importing goods once again from England. The students felt this letter was a blow to the growing American desire for independence from Great Britain. Madison joined the other students at Princeton in a protest. They all dressed in black and marched outside Nassau Hall. A hangman they had hired then burned a copy of the letter to the tolling of a bell.

As graduation drew near, Madison's health grew worse, perhaps due to his overstudy and lack of sleep. Madison had some serious illnesses and many bouts of a nervous disorder that left him exhausted. He also suffered from hypochondria and believed that he would not live long or have a healthy life. Perhaps for these reasons, he was the only graduating senior who did not take part in the commencement ceremonies.

After Madison graduated in September of 1771, he received his father's permission to do graduate study under President Witherspoon. Madison stayed on for six months, taught solely by President Witherspoon. He learned some Hebrew, which had not been part of the college curriculum. He continued to read John Locke, David Hume, and others who shaped the Enlightenment worldview. Madison also studied some books on law and theology. In the spring of 1772, Madison left Princeton and returned to the family estate. His former tutor, Thomas Martin, had died, and his father needed another tutor for the younger Madison children. James Madison decided to fill that role.

Leaving Princeton did not end the education of James Madison. In fact, during the next three years he added greatly to his knowledge. His first responsibility was the teaching of his youngest siblings. However, he had a great deal of time to read, study, and meditate. He wanted to keep learning and to use his time for developing his understanding of the world. As he corresponded with his former college friend, William Bradford, they exchanged lists of books they wanted to have for their libraries.

Madison did a great deal of study in the New Testament, taking notes on William Burkett's book *Expository Notes*, which had been recently purchased by his father. He did not consider the Christian ministry as a career, but he did say that divinity was the most sublime of all sciences. He encouraged William Bradford to "season his other studies with a little divinity now and then, which like the philosopher's stone…will turn them…into the nature of itself and make them more precious than gold."

In this page from the minutes for 1771, the Board of Trustees raised student fees in order to make repairs to their living quarters. The Trustees also appointed William Churchill Houston as professor of mathematics and natural philosophy (science). Houston graduated from Princeton in 1768 and remained there first as master of the college grammar school and then as a tutor. Houston was Madison's tutor in 1770. Subsequently, Houston became a revolutionary leader as captain of the Somerset County, New Jersey, militia (1776), deputy secretary of the Continental Congress (1775–76), and a delegate to the Constitutional Convention (1787).

The study of government was a subject that increasingly interested Madison. He felt that the principles and forms of modern governments were too important to be ignored by anyone who had a thirst for knowledge. As he studied privately at Montpelier, he was well aware of the abuses of the government in Virginia. The established Episcopal Church persecuted anyone who disagreed with its doctrines. Five Baptist ministers were in jail for publishing their religious ideas, even though they were accepted Christian teachings. Frustrated over the oppressive atmosphere in Virginia, he wrote to Bradford in Pennsylvania, "I want again to breathe your free air."

Madison's political life began in 1774 when he was elected to the Committee of Safety in Orange County, chaired by his father. In 1776, he was elected a member of the Virginia House of Delegates, where he met Thomas Jefferson for the first time. The two began a friendship that lasted the rest of their lives. Madison worked hard to enact Jefferson's bill for religious freedom. Madison also worked closely with Jefferson and Patrick Henry for the independence of the Virginia colony. After the revolution he was a member of the Virginia House of Delegates and opposed the reestablishment of the Episcopal Church in Virginia. He was able to defeat all attempts to use tax money to support any Christian denomination in the newly formed State of Virginia.

The Princeton University archives have a complete record of the Board of Trustees minutes, a few dating back to the founding of the college in 1746. However, the military campaigns fought during the American Revolution in and around Princeton, and subsequent fires, destroyed most of the early college records.

This entry of June 26, 1860, is interesting because it explains how commencement exercises were held. The board ordered the procedure to be the same as the previous year: "The candidates for the first degree in the Arts, with the exception of Valedictory orator, delivered their speeches in the morning of Wednesday, the day of Commencement. There was then an intermission in the exercises for an hour. After which the Master's Oration was pronounced, the degrees were conferred and the Valedictory addresses were made. The whole exercises were concluded with prayer and with a benediction. The permission for music is the same as it was last year, and the expense will be the same, vig. one hundred and twenty-five dollars."

The president of the Board of Trustees also noted "with pleasure" that the buildings of the college and the surrounding grounds were maintained in excellent condition. He also announced that Nassau Hall had been rebuilt after the 1855 fires and he offered a prayer for its completion "without the loss of a single life, and without any serious or lasting injury. Let us be thankful."

The Board of Trustees accepted the gift of the late Professor Matthew B. Hope's 1,600-volume library. Hope was remembered by graduates of that period as one of Princeton's most inspiring teachers.

Before Jefferson went to Paris in 1785, he agreed to buy a number of books for Madison, particularly those that concerned ancient and modern republics. Jefferson also sent Madison thirty-seven volumes of the *Encyclopedie Methodique,* which Madison described as a complete scientific library. He pored over these books to learn the history of European nations and to discover the strengths and weaknesses of their governments.

In 1787, Madison was elected a delegate to the Constitutional Convention. It was here that his skills in political science and logic would become evident. Because of his great involvement in the debates surrounding the Constitution, and his work to have the document approved, Madison is often called the Father of the Constitution. His extensive notes and journals are the principal sources of information about the convention and the process of drafting the Constitution.

Madison was determined to help create a strong central government that would last. Once the Constitution was written, he wanted to make sure it would be approved by the people. He wrote a number of essays about the Constitution, explaining the document and encouraging the states to ratify it. Madison's essays, along with similar essays by John Jay and Alexander Hamilton, became known as the Federalist Papers. These influential essays convinced Americans to approve the Constitution. It became the basis for the U.S. government in 1789.

Madison was elected to the House of Representatives from Virginia in 1789. He continued his work in establishing the new government and sponsored the first ten amendments to the Constitution—the Bill of Rights.

Marriage came late for James Madison. He met a widow, Dorothea "Dolley" Payne Todd, when he was forty-three and married her on September 15, 1794. Dolley Madison became a charming first lady when Madison became president in 1809.

Madison was secretary of state for eight years under President Thomas Jefferson, then served two terms as president. He retired on March 4, 1817, and returned to Montpelier. He continued to receive new books, as well as newspapers and reports from political, educational, and scientific organizations. Madison wrote articles and letters, and spent a great deal of time organizing his own papers. He also served as rector of the University of Virginia from 1826 to 1836.

Madison was described in his retirement by one visitor as a man who "sparkled in conversation," who had a remarkable command of the English language, and was profound and far-reaching in his views. Even when he was unable to read in his old age, Dolley would sit at his side and read for him. His mind never stopped searching for knowledge. He died peacefully on June 28, 1836, at the age of eighty-five.

Throughout James Madison's life, he always acknowledged the importance of education, particularly as it related to government. In a letter to his friend W. T. Barry, dated August 4, 1822, he wrote: "A popular government without popular information, or the means of acquiring it, is but a prologue to a farce or a tragedy, or perhaps both. Knowledge will forever govern ignorance, and a people who mean to be their own governors must arm themselves with the power which knowledge gives."

—Bill Thompson

James Monroe
Chapter Five

It was a hot, difficult march for James Monroe, a young college student from Virginia. It was late summer of 1776, and he had enlisted in the military and was joining several hundred other men heading for New York. When they arrived on the island of Manhattan with the other troops from Virginia, he and the others were exhausted. However, their spirits were high because they were anxious to face the British army. The Virginians joined General George Washington's men already camped at Harlem and settled in. Just a few days later, word came that the British had invaded Manhattan just six miles south of the Americans. Monroe waited with the Continental army for the British advance north.

Monroe was furious when he heard that poorly trained troops from Connecticut had run from the British without offering any resistance. He wanted the English to arrive so he and his fellow soldiers could show them the courage of Virginia men. When the British did reach Harlem, the fresh Virginia infantry held back the strong and continuous British attacks. The next day, General Washington honored the young men from Virginia for their bravery. He was especially impressed by the courage of the broad-shouldered, six-foot-tall Monroe.

This experience of warfare was a world away from the life that James Monroe had known in Virginia, four hundred miles south of the Harlem battlefield. Monroe was born in Westmoreland County on April 28, 1758. His home in Westmoreland County, between the Potomac and Rappahannock Rivers, was not far from where George Washington had spent his youth. James was the oldest son of Spence and Elizabeth Monroe, whose ancestors had settled there more than a century before his birth.

Early colonists had first farmed the fertile soil of Virginia on the peninsula where Westmoreland County was located. Raising tobacco was hard on the soil, so every three or four years a planter would have to move to new fields and let the older land lay fallow. By the time Monroe was born, the soil of Westmoreland County had become poor through over cultivation, and the land was profitable only to those great Virginia families that owned thousands of acres.

The time that James Monroe spent at William and Mary (1774–76) coincided with the most disruptive period in the college's history. William and Mary was identified with the Church of England, the state religion. By 1775, at the outset of the Revolution, many American-based Anglican ministers, including two of the six college professors (a third was in London for his ordination), took up the Tory cause.

In this September 14, 1775, entry from the Journal of the Meetings of the President and Masters, the Reverend John Camm, the Loyalist president of William and Mary, dismissed James Innes from his position as head usher of the grammar school. (An usher would be equivalent to a college tutor today—somewhere between a student and a faculty member.) Innes was accused of "neglecting his Duty for the three last months by repeatedly absenting himself from the College for days & weeks together, without asking permission to be absent, behaving herein as if he had no superior in the Society to whom he thought himself accountable for his conduct." At the bottom of this entry is the cryptic admonition: "No Arms or Ammunition shall be brought into the College and kept there by the students."

James Innes had entered William and Mary in 1771. By 1775, he had become the captain of the Williamsburg volunteers and therefore an anathema to the Tory college president. In his five years as an undergraduate and usher—the five years that led up to the Revolution—Innes was not only eager for the fighting against the British to begin but he also was determined to enlist his fellow students in the revolutionary cause. Innes was extremely popular, except with the college leaders. As an usher living in the ambiguous world between faculty and undergraduates, Innes aroused agitation among the students and anguish among his professors.

Innes influenced young James Monroe. He encouraged Monroe's decision to leave William and Mary and join the Williamsburg volunteers. This decision affected the rest of Monroe's life.

War disrupts the College of William and Mary

In 1774, at age sixteen, James Monroe entered the College of William and Mary. But the advent of the American Revolution soon interrupted his academic studies. In 1776, at age eighteen, he enlisted in a Virginia regiment of the Continental Army.

Students at the College of William and Mary were absorbed by the crisis with Great Britain, as was the rest of America. Yet, routine continued. Solemn young men attended meetings of earnest societies to debate philosophical issues. Reverend William Henley, a professor of moral philosophy who was the most popular of the faculty members, gave lectures on the "Elementary Ideas of Poetry" to those gentlemen of Williamsburg who chose to pay a fee to attend. Whenever he spoke, the Great Hall at the college was usually filled to capacity.

However, Henley opposed the Revolution. An American bishop in an independent United States, he reasoned, would weaken the connection to the Church of England. The relationship, he wrote, would be no better than "a Mongrel Episcopate." In late 1775, after the outbreak of war, Henley left Virginia for England, where he lived for the next forty years.

By coincidence, Henley later taught George Gordon, Lord Byron, at Harrow, an English boarding school for boys that had been founded in 1571. During the last years of Henley's life, his former student Monroe was secretary of state and secretary of war of the United States, which at the time was fighting Great Britain in the War of 1812. At the same time, Lord Byron had become Britain's most famous man of letters.

Although he could trace his ancestry to British royalty, Spence Monroe had inherited only five hundred acres of land and was not a wealthy man. Yet, he was still considered part of the gentry, or ruling class, although he was at the lower end of the social ladder. None of the Monroe ancestors had been able to afford college. Few had held important political positions, because Virginia's government was run by members of wealthy families with large landholdings: the Carters, the Randolphs, the Byrds, and the Lees. However, James's mother, Elizabeth Jones Monroe, came from a wealthier family. Her brother, Joseph Jones, was an important judge in Fredericksburg. He would prove to be a powerful asset to James Monroe as the young man matured.

James grew up in a world of agriculture and for the rest of his life he loved being close to the soil where he felt a sense of peace. He lived near the major north-south road that connected Williamsburg, the Virginia capital, with a ferry that crossed the Potomac. As a result, even when he was a boy James was well informed about the political events of his day.

Like all of the children of the gentry, James began his education at home. His first teachers were his parents, who taught him to read and write. His mother was an educated woman, unusual for the time. From his early years, however, James's education developed as much through experience as through formal schooling. When he was seven, he watched as his father organized a boycott with a hundred other Westmoreland County men against the Stamp Act of 1765. The British had put a tax on all paper used by the colonists for official documents, a decision deeply resented throughout the colonies. James saw how effective the protest was when the British repealed the Stamp Act a year later.

When James was eleven years old, he started to attend his first formal school, Campbelltown Academy, where he studied from 1769 to 1774. It was considered the best grammar school in Virginia. Monroe later wrote, "Twenty-five students only were admitted into his academy, but so high was its character that youths were sent to it from more distant parts of the then colony." The founder of the school, and its teacher, was the Reverend Archibald Campbell, who was then rector of Washington Parish, where the Monroe family lived and worshiped.

Reverend Campbell had come to Virginia from Scotland in 1741 and had established his academy about nine years later. He was called "a clergyman of great respectability" and was known for his learning, especially his knowledge of Greek studies. Reverend Campbell was also called "a disciplinarian of the sternest type" and did not allow the students much time for play. He was an excellent teacher and emphasized mathematics and Latin.

Monroe's father had gone to the academy, as had most of the children of the gentry in Westmoreland. When James Monroe first began his studies, he developed a close friendship with young John Marshall, and the two would remain lifelong friends The boys undoubtedly found ways to have fun together in spite of their strict teacher. Eventually they both became lawyers in Richmond (Marshall would eventually become chief justice of the U.S. Supreme Court) and, as adults, loved to play cards and billiards together and went to the theatre as often as possible.

While at Campbelltown, Monroe learned Latin and Greek and received a well-grounded classical education. He read Pope's "Essay on Man" and some of his "Moral Essays." As Monroe continued his studies, the political situation in the colonies was becoming increasingly unstable. Boycotts and demonstrations were common. In 1773, Boston citizens dumped tea in the harbor and defied British authority. The students heard the citizens of Westmoreland County openly speaking against England.

Both of Monroe's parents died within months of each other in 1774, leaving James as heir of the Monroe estate. His father's death left him with the responsibility for the welfare of his two brothers, Andrew and Joseph, as well as his sister Elizabeth. Fortunately for James Monroe, his uncle, Judge Jones, was executor of the estate. The Judge was a wealthy man and a member of the House of Burgesses, the Virginia legislature, which made him part of the group that ruled Virginia. The Joneses had no children and treated teenage James as their own son.

Judge Jones believed Monroe was ready for advanced education. Both James and his uncle had hoped that James could go to Europe for his studies. Most children of the gentry went to England for advanced schooling, because this was considered superior to the educational opportunities available in colonial America. However, the political situation made that difficult. With his uncle's connections,

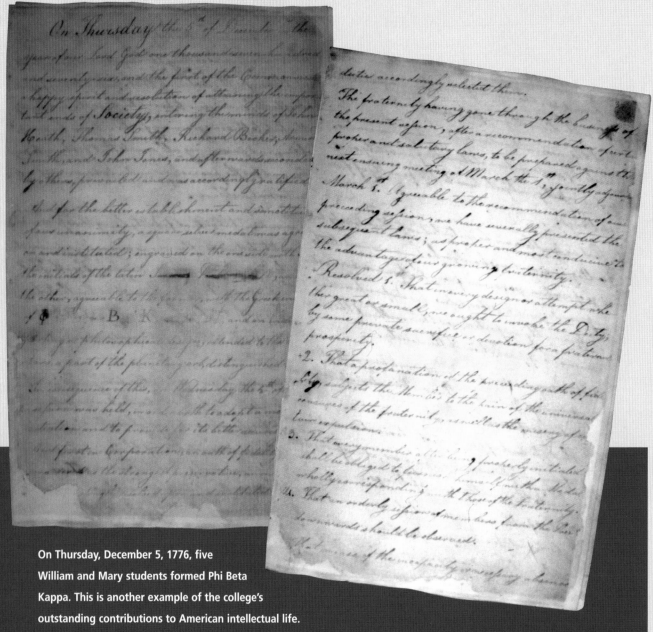

On Thursday, December 5, 1776, five William and Mary students formed Phi Beta Kappa. This is another example of the college's outstanding contributions to American intellectual life.

The entry from the first two pages of the minute book of Phi Beta Kappa (pictured above) reads in part, "On Thursdy, the 5th of December, in the year of our Lord God one thousand seven hundred and seventy-six, and the first of the Commonwealth, a happy spirit and resolution of attaining the important ends of Society entering the minds of John Heath, Thomas Smith, Richard Booker, Armstd Smith, and John Jones, and afterwards seconded by others, prevailed, and was accordingly ratified.

"And for the better establishment and sanctitude of our unanimity, a square silver medal was agreed on and instituted, engraved on the one side with S.P., the initials of the Latin S[ocietas] P[hilosophas], and on the other, agreeable to the former, with the Greek initials FBK, and an index imparting a philosophical design, extended to the three stars, a part of the planetary orb, distinguished."

Phi Beta Kappa was the first undergraduate secret society at an American college. It began as a social fraternity, but has evolved to become the leading advocate of the liberal arts and sciences at the undergraduate level. Today, Phi Beta Kappa elects more than 15,000 new members annually from its nearly 270 chapters across the United States. Membership is open to both men and women undergraduates who excel in academics.

and probably with his financial support as well, sixteen-year-old Monroe went to Williamsburg in June of 1774 to attend the College of William and Mary.

James Monroe did very well in his entrance exams, which included the classical materials he had studied under Campbell. Monroe soon discovered, however, that he was in an entirely new environment. All of his life he had lived among planters, who generally opposed the authority of the British crown. Now Monroe found himself in a school where some of the professors were Tories who supported the authority of the British crown.

Monroe was introduced to his roommate, John Mercer, who was fifteen and came from a wealthy family. The two became good friends and started their classes together. Both were immediately affected, however, by the political developments in Williamsburg. Not long after Monroe and his roommate began their studies, the governor of Virginia, John Murray, the Earl of Dunmore, tried to show his authority by dissolving the Virginia House of Burgesses.

The burgesses continued to assemble, meeting instead in the Apollo Room of Raleigh Tavern, just down the street from the college. They met twice that summer in opposition to the governor. Monroe was especially aware of the conflict because his uncle, Joseph Jones, was one of the burgesses. Both students and faculty at William and Mary discussed the clash between the governor and the burgesses. For a while, teaching and studying took a backseat to politics.

When the struggle quieted, Monroe returned to his studies. Only sixteen, he discovered that he was not fully prepared for the work he was asked to do. Some years later, Monroe wrote to a nephew about his first six months at the college: "I had been examined…and [was] found well qualified to enter the philosophical school." But when he began his advanced mathematics course, Monroe discovered, "I was altogether unqualified" and "made a ridiculous figure." When his winter vacation came, Monroe decided to stay on in Williamsburg and use that time for intense study. When he returned to the classroom after two months, "I had made such good use of my time that I obtained the approbation and praise of the professors."

Through the first part of 1775, the College of William and Mary went about the business of education. Then in April, the governor again created a crisis. He sent soldiers to seize some gunpowder that belonged to the city of Williamsburg. Some patriots discovered the plan, and bands of men gathered to protect the powder. Governor Dunmore agreed to pay for it, calming some of the citizens. However, the whole matter aroused the college students, and they began to join townspeople at frequent meetings being held throughout the city. Monroe went to these meetings and joined other students as they spent time drilling on the college campus.

During that same time, a twenty-year-old worker at the college, James Innes, spoke openly on campus about the need to arm. He created a military group of interested students; Monroe was impressed by him and joined the militia. Like many other students, Monroe purchased a rifle and kept it in his room against school rules. Innes was considered a nuisance in the eyes of the college professors.

He was accused of taking students to a tavern, getting them drunk, and causing a disturbance late at night. Finally, in June 1775 Innes left the college and went to fight in the new Continental Army, much to the relief of the faculty.

Also in June 1775, a British general met with the burgesses and tried to work out a compromise with them. They remained defiant, however, and Governor Dunmore, concerned by some of their radical comments, sought refuge in a British warship on the James River. The burgesses quickly set up a committee to take over the government of the capital. Fighting broke out between the British soldiers and the citizens of Williamsburg.

After the British army fired on militiamen at Concord, Massachusetts, Monroe joined a group of twenty-four men, made up of college students and older males, and attacked the Governor's palace on June 24. At seventeen, Monroe was the youngest member of the group. There was no resistance at the palace, and the rebel band easily walked off with two hundred muskets and three hundred swords. The weapons were donated to the Virginia militia.

In spite of his involvement in these military adventures, Monroe continued in his studies. The colonists began to take over the entire Virginia colony over the next year, and throughout the American colonies people were preparing for war. Monroe knew he had to make a choice. In the spring of 1776, Monroe and his roommate, John Mercer decided to suspend their college careers and join the patriot cause. They enlisted, along with other students from William and Mary, in the Third Virginia Regiment. They were made lieutenants and joined in the long march toward Washington's army camped on the island of Manhattan. However, if Monroe thought he was leaving his studies behind, he would discover that opportunities to learn were everywhere.

After the battle at Manhattan, Monroe was among Washington's troops as they retreated through New Jersey. The American army reached the Delaware River by December. When Washington decided to attack Trenton on Christmas Day, Monroe was with a group of fifty men who were sent ahead toward the city. Monroe was seriously wounded at Trenton and spent three months recovering in Bucks County, Pennsylvania. He eventually rejoined Washington and when the Continental Army was camped at Valley Forge during the next winter, Monroe shared a cabin with his old friend, John Marshall, who had also enlisted.

Monroe felt that the many new relationships he was making in the military were valuable, because they gave him a greater knowledge of other parts of the world. He realized that when his experience was limited only to Virginia, his perspective on events had been limited also.

One of the men who most influenced Monroe during this time was Pierre S. DuPonceau, an eighteen-year-old from France. The young Frenchman was highly intelligent and spoke excellent English. He began to share with Monroe the writings of French philosophers, subjects Monroe had never studied. The two young men had the same interest in reading and shared books with one another. They had long talks about what they were reading and became extremely close.

Front and back views of the oldest extant Phi Beta Kappa key, which was given to William Short in 1780.

Short attended William and Mary from 1777 to 1781, and was the president of the society from 1778 to 1781. After leaving the college, he had a distinguished career in government. Short was Thomas Jefferson's private secretary during his mission to France, 1785–87. From Paris, Jefferson, John Adams, and Benjamin Franklin sent Short to The Hague to meet with a Prussian envoy and arrange a commercial treaty between Prussia and the United States. Short also served as minister to the Netherlands, 1792–93.

DuPonceau gave Monroe popular plays by Nicholas Rowe, who incorporated politics throughout his dramas. The Frenchman also loaned Monroe sermons by preacher James Watson, who had liberal ideas on Christianity. DuPonceau encouraged Monroe to read books by French philosopher Mark Akenside, who placed ancient Greek ideas above those of the Christian faith. This period of study gave Monroe a broader concept of the war against Great Britain. He came to believe that he was involved in a battle to free *all* humankind from oppression.

When it became apparent that he would not receive a field command, Monroe resigned from the army on December 20, 1778, and returned to Virginia. For a year he tried to find a position in the Virginia state militia but could not. He met and became friends with Thomas Jefferson, who had become governor of Virginia in 1779. Jefferson appreciated the warmth and sincerity of the young former soldier and became his mentor. Through Jefferson's friendship, a new period of education began for the twenty-one-year-old Monroe. Jefferson encouraged Monroe to study law as a way of entering politics and helping to develop the new nation.

In 1780, Monroe "submitted the direction of his studies" to Jefferson and reentered William and Mary as his apprentice. Jefferson was interested in helping his apprentices learn the basic principles of law. Monroe and two other young men began to study the writings of a liberal lawmaker, Edward Coke, and a famous English jurist, Sir William Blackstone. The young apprentices were allowed to study the law cases of Jefferson and were given the large collection of the statutes of Virginia to read.

The final stage of their apprenticeship was to read the great books of western civilization, both ancient and modern. Among them were the writings of the philosopher and historian David Hume, the English philosopher John Locke, and the French philosopher Jean Rousseau. Ancient authors included the Greek moralist Plutarch, the Roman historian Tacitus, and the Greek stoic Epictetus.

Monroe's gratitude to Jefferson was expressed in a letter he wrote to his teacher in September 1780:

> Your kindness and attention to me in this and variety of other instances has really put me under such obligations to you that I fear I shall hardly ever have it in my power to repay them....You became acquainted with me and undertook the direction of my studies and believe me I feel that whatever I am at present in the opinion of others or whatever I may be in future has greatly arise from your friendship. My plan of life is now fixed, [and] has a certain object for its view…

Monroe expected to study next with the famous Virginia lawyer, George Wythe, Jefferson's early teacher in Williamsburg. Wythe had recently become a law professor at William and Mary, and Monroe looked forward to learning from him. However, Jefferson told Monroe he was moving to Richmond, Virginia, where the capital had been relocated, and invited Monroe to go with him. Monroe sought advice from his uncle, who encouraged him to continue his association with Jefferson. Monroe went with Jefferson and shortly after settled down on an estate not far from Richmond. There he continued the study of law, still under Jefferson's tutelage.

By October of 1781, Monroe had finished the books Jefferson had given him and made plans to go to Europe to complete his education. He wrote to Jefferson, "Since my return from Richmond I have…read all the books you mention of the subject of law." He was interested, he wrote Jefferson, not only to study for the sake of being able to practice law, but also to better himself. What could be acquired from books, Monroe wrote, "will qualify a man not only for public office, but enable him to bear prosperity or adversity…by giving him resources within himself, of pleasure and content which otherwise he would look for in vain from others."

Monroe was not able to go, however. The next spring, with the fighting of the American Revolution ended, he was elected to the House of Delegates from

King George County. His political career had begun. Monroe became a member of the Continental Congress in 1783 and a U.S. Senator in 1790. He finally traveled to Europe when he became minister to France in 1794.

In 1785, while a member of the Continental Congress, Monroe met Elizabeth Kortright, only sixteen years old but "a statuesque beauty with raven hair and blue eyes." They were married a year later, on February 16, 1786, and had two daughters.

Monroe's career continued without a break. He was governor of Virginia twice, minister to Great Britain, secretary of state and secretary of war. He was elected president in 1816 (the first president to have been a senator) and again in 1820. Monroe retired on March 4, 1825, and moved into a new home, Oak Hill, in Virginia. When his wife died in 1830, he went to live with a daughter and son-in-law in New York City.

President James Monroe died in New York on July 4, 1831. He was the third president to die on the anniversary of the Declaration of Independence.

James Monroe's public career was greatly influenced by three major factors: the American Revolution; the principles of the Republican Party, which he helped found (this party eventually evolved into the Democratic Party); and his diplomatic experiences. The Monroe Doctrine was one of the most important principles in U.S. foreign policy, as it closed the Americas to further colonization by European powers like France, Spain, and Great Britain.

Perhaps one of the best remarks to be made about James Monroe was spoken about him while he was still in his twenties. Thomas Jefferson said "Turn his soul wrong side outwards and there is not a speck on it."

—Bill Thompson

John Quincy Adams
Chapter Six

Imagine a twelve-year-old giving language lessons to a French ambassador. This happened to young John Quincy Adams aboard a ship, *La Sensible*, soon after it sailed out of the French port of Nantes. Just one year in France had helped John Quincy, who was then called Johnny, learn French. He was traveling with his father, John Adams, to their home in Quincy, Massachusetts. Another passenger on *La Sensible* was Chevalier Anne Cesar de La Luzerne, the new French ambassador to the United States.

John Adams entered the lounge of the ship one day and found Johnny sitting with the French ambassador. Next to them was the ambassador's private secretary. John Adams could see that the two men were fascinated by his son. They were reading aloud a lecture by an English jurist, Sir William Blackstone. Their English was rather poor, and Johnny was correcting each word and syllable they spoke. He was giving them no praise for their efforts and showed little sympathy for their mistakes.

Rather than resent this, the two Frenchmen told John Adams that they could not do without his son, "little John." He was an enormous help to them in learning the English language, and they were grateful that he used no flattery and was firm with them. John Adams was pleased that his son had been able to help them. Young Johnny Adams, one day to become the sixth president of the United States, was a unique young person who experienced an unusual childhood.

John Quincy Adams was born in Quincy (then Braintree), Massachusetts, on July 11, 1767. Johnny lived with his parents, Abigail and John, in a frame house just across the street from where his father had lived as a boy. He had an older sister, Abigail (Nabby), and two younger brothers, Charles and Tom. John Adams practiced law and had his offices in the front room of their home. Johnny enjoyed the same kind of early boyhood as his father and grandfather had. He loved to walk through the marshes, to hunt in the wooded hills, and to fish in the streams flowing into the nearby bay.

Education was a priority in the Adam's household. Both Abigail and John Adams were dedicated to passing on to their children their own love of learning and of books. They taught Johnny to read and write by the time he was five, and by

March 20, 1778.

being a Committee appointed by the said Corporation

The Subscribers, having examined the Steward's accounts of disbursements for commons from Nov. 14. 1777 to March 12. 1778 inclusively, beg leave to represent to the Reverend Corporation that they find,

That the Steward had stores remaining on hand Nov. 14. 1777 — — — — £ 99.15.0

That in the time above specified he purchased provisions to the amount of — 609 . 8. 11

That he has received from the College wood-lot fourteen loads of wood a 60/ 42 : 0 . 0
Also one load of faggots 1.10. 0

That there must be charged for wear of table-linen — — — — — — — — 4. 10. 0

That no charge be allowed for the Laundress this quarter because a full allowance was made the last quarter, and the students were dismissed as many days before the last quarter-day, as they have been convened before the present —

That from the above sum there must be deducted 757 . 3. 11
as follows for provisions charged as settings 26.16.1¾
Stores unexpended — — — — 309. — — 335:16. 1¾

That the neat expense for provisions is — 421. 7. 9¾

Examination of the Harvard steward's accounts, March 20, 1778.

This committee reviewed the Harvard steward's account book. Among other things, it was noted that there was no laundry charge between November 1777 and March 1778 as "the students were dismissed as many days before the last quarter-day, as they have been convened." The Continental Army had sent General Burgoyne's surrendered troops to be housed in the college buildings. This caused most classes to be cancelled during the winter 1777–78 term.

Schedule of the debt due the Harvard steward, September 12, 1777.

The steward was in charge of food and drink served to the students. By the 1770s, Harvard had scholarships to pay all or part of a student's expenses based on need. It is estimated that £30 a year covered the board and lodging of a poorer student. However, the usual cost was much higher. One father estimated that his son's Harvard education in 1769 cost about £55 per year in specie.

the time he was six he was expected to write letters. However, though Johnny participated in the normal activities for a boy his age, he was also exposed to the conflicts that were occurring between the British and the American colonists. That struggle, which led to the Revolutionary War, greatly affected John Quincy Adams's upbringing and early education.

Colonial resistance to British authority was beginning to break into physical violence while Johnny was very young. His father had taken the family to live in Boston as his law practice began to prosper. During the winter of 1770, British troops fired on a mob not far from their home, killing five colonists. This skirmish became known as the Boston Massacre. John Adams was the only lawyer who would defend the British soldiers, for which some people scorned him. As a result of the unrest in Boston, in early 1771 John moved his wife and children back to the farm in Quincy, eleven miles south of Boston. The family returned to Boston in 1772, but after further troubles with the British they returned to Quincy to stay.

Much of Johnny's early education was left to Abigail because John was busy establishing his legal practice. He later became involved in the colonies' fight for independence from Britain. Because of that, he spent much time in Philadelphia as a member of the Continental Congress. Though absent from home, his letters to Abigail expressed his concerns for the education of his family. "Above all cares of this life let our ardent anxiety be to improve the minds and manners of our children," he wrote. "Let us teach them not only to do virtuously, but to excel."

The political situation in Massachusetts grew worse in 1775, and Abigail became anxious about the education of her children. Public schools were not operating, and she had to find other ways to teach Johnny. Her husband had two law clerks, John Thaxter and Nathan Rice, who became Johnny's tutors for a time. Johnny especially liked Thaxter, his father's cousin, who helped Johnny with some of the basics, such as Latin, which he had started learning from by his parents. John Adams helped by writing regularly from Philadelphia and including Latin sentences for Johnny to translate.

Abigail watched over Johnny's progress and asked him to read to her from Rollin's *Ancient History*, a text that had been translated from French. In his letters, John Adams encouraged Abigail to make sure Johnny was taught geography and the skill of copying, which was then considered essential to learning. Johnny developed a daily schedule of reading that included the *Complete History of England* by Tobias Smollett. John Adams also wrote directly to his oldest son, challenging him to prepare to learn Greek. He wanted him to have the pleasure one day of reading the *History of the Peloponnesian War* by historian Thucydides in the original Greek.

Bible reading was a regular practice for everyone in the family, and John Quincy developed a habit of reading the Bible for an hour each day. He also loved fairy tales and pored over the *Arabian Nights*. For Johnny, the characters in the stories seemed to be real people. He read many Shakespeare plays, such as *The Tempest, As You Like It,* and *Much Ado About Nothing.* Reading them made him feel as though he was in an enchanted world. He tried to understand *Paradise Lost* by John Milton, because his parents both loved it. Johnny did not finish reading this difficult epic poem, though, until he had become an adult.

One day in the spring of 1775, Abigail and the children climbed Penn's Hill behind their home, where they could look north toward Boston. They saw the city of Charlestown in flames—it had been set on fire by British troops. Another day, from the same spot, they heard the roar of cannon from a battle on Breeds Hill just outside Boston. (This battle became popularly, though erroneously, known as the Battle of Bunker Hill.) Because of John Adams's position in the Continental Congress, Abigail and her children feared that one day British soldiers might snatch them from their home and take them hostage into Boston. In spite of their anxieties, both Abigail and John instilled strong patriotic feelings in their four children. Abigail had Johnny memorize "How Sleep the Brave," a heroic poem honoring warriors who had died in battle. He quoted it every day after he said the Lord's Prayer.

Realizing that Johnny's education had been severely interrupted by the confusion of war, Abigail was determined to send him to the Governor Dummer

Academy, north of Boston. This would prepare him to enter Harvard College, the school from which his father had graduated. However, in November 1777 Congress asked her husband to be a member of a commission being sent to France to win its support for the American cause. John Thaxter suggested that Johnny travel with his father because he would learn much from the experience. With the approval of Abigail and John, ten-year-old Johnny was at his father's side as the ship *Boston* sailed out of Massachusetts Bay on February 13, 1778.

For three days and nights the *Boston* was tossed around by a severe hurricane, making John Adams regret that he had brought his young son. Though strong winds continued throughout the voyage, Johnny handled it well and even used the time for study. A French surgeon on the ship, Dr. Nicholas Noel, took a liking to Johnny and began teaching him French. At other times, Johnny wandered the ship and spent time with the captain, who taught him about the compass, about navigation, and how to work the sails of the *Boston*.

At the end of March, the ship had reached the coast of France. The passengers left the storm-battered ship at Bordeaux on April 1. After several days, John Adams and his son continued on to Paris and reached the bustling city on April 8. Both Adamses were impressed by the sights and sounds of Paris, which was so much larger than Boston. Johnny was placed in a boarding school in Passy, a suburb of Paris, along with several other American boys, including Benjamin Franklin's grandson. This was Johnny's first formal school education. The academy was run by M. LeCoeur, who emphasized French and Latin. Johnny also learned fencing, dancing, drawing, and music, subjects not considered important back home in Massachusetts.

The students began school each morning at 6 A.M. At 8 A.M. they had a break for breakfast and then went to class again from 9 A.M. to noon. There was another break for dinner and play, followed by afternoon classes from 2 P.M. until 4:30 P.M. The students had thirty minutes for play and then took their final classes from 5 P.M. until 7:30 P.M. They ate supper and played games before going to bed at 9 P.M. The only day off was Sunday, when they attended church. In spite of the busy schedule, Johnny loved the school and learned to speak and write the French language with much greater fluency than his father.

Johnny turned eleven that summer and began to develop a love for the theater, particularly comedies. Johnny had begun to keep a diary so that he would remember the things he was experiencing. His diary and letters home were filled with the names of famous actors and with the titles of Shakespeare plays he had attended. Although Abigail was concerned about his morals—she wrote to Johnny that he should be careful—John Adams replied to his wife that she did not have to worry, because Johnny was a good student and well-behaved.

The Commission was having little success in France, and at the end of 1778 Congress decided to recall the commissioners. The two Adamses left Paris at the beginning of March 1779 and prepared to head home. They had difficulty finding a ship to take them back to America and spent three months together reading

Harvard During and After the American Revolution

The American Revolution (1775–81) brought profound change to Harvard College. The overwhelming number of students, faculty, and alumni opposed Great Britain and sided with the revolutionaries. Under the leadership of John Hancock, whose titles also included treasurer of Harvard, the Second Massachusetts Provincial Congress met at Cambridge in February 1775. They framed measures to prepare the colony for war. Of the 1,224 Harvard graduates living on January 1, 1776, only 196 (16 percent) were loyalists.

Numerous battles between the British and the Massachusetts militia—and later the Continental Army—occurred in Massachusetts between April 1775 and March 1776, when the British evacuated Boston. More than a thousand militiamen were quartered in the college. Half a ton of lead from the roofs was molded into bullets. Brass knobs and box locks disappeared. Some buildings never recovered and were eventually torn down. Within days of British General Sir William Howe's decision to evacuate Boston, taking with him about a thousand loyalists, the Harvard Corporation conferred on General George Washington an honorary doctor of laws degree.

The college labored under great difficulty during the war. Student enrollment fell off: from 1778 through 1783 the average size of the graduating classes was thirty students, compared to an average class of forty-six during the period 1771 to 1777. Trade and transportation were so disrupted that it was often difficult to obtain supplies for the college community. One student wrote home in 1777 that the steward never knew one day if he would have food for the commons the next day. The textbook shortage became so acute that in 1778 the college president petitioned the State of Massachusetts for the authority to plunder sequestered Tory libraries for books. During the winter of 1777–78, the students had to be sent home because the college buildings were needed as prisons to house the British soldiers captured in the surrender of General John Burgoyne's army after the Battle of Saratoga. Very few members of the Harvard war classes attained distinction.

Equally startling was the tolerance of college authorities toward irregularities during this time. Students slipped away for a year or more and returned to their old standing without examination or a "make up," provided they paid the college fees for the period of their absence. One "student" appeared at Cambridge for the first time on July 18, 1780, passed examinations in seven subjects, paid two years' tuition, and obtained his bachelor's degree the following day. In the summer of 1780, a group of students told President Samuel Langdon, "As a man of genius and knowledge we respect you; as a man of piety and virtue we venerate you; as a President we despise you." Langdon resigned.

Eighteen-year-old John Quincy Adams entered Harvard with advanced standing in October 1785. He already had been the private secretary to the American minister to Russia in St. Petersburg (1781), and to his father, statesman John Adams, in Great Britain (1782–83). He had traveled widely in Europe, often on his own. He had attended a Paris boarding school with Benjamin Franklin's grandson and studied at a Latin school in Amsterdam. With his mother Abigail, he shared the delights of the French theater. He knew Latin and Greek, and he spoke French, Dutch, and German. He also had met many of the leading cultural and political European figures of the day. His father, himself a Harvard graduate (Class of 1755), wrote from London congratulating John Quincy on his admission "into the seat of the Muses, our dear Alma Mater, where I hope you will find a Pleasure and Improvements equal to your Expectations."

Adams was a serious student. He wrote to his sister that in his first year at Harvard, he had to relearn his Greek grammar, study the New Testament, read four of the eight books in Xenophon's *Cyropedia* (which describes the education of the ideal ruler) and five or six books in Homer's *Iliad.* "In Latin," Adams wrote, "I have but little else to go through but Horace, part of which I have already done. In English, I have to study Watts' Logic, Locke on the Human Understanding, and something in Astronomy."

Joseph Willard, the college president, enforced authority and standards. He wore a white wig and a black gown. Students were expected to take off their hats when the president entered Harvard Yard. Students wore a blue-gray coat, with a vest, and black or olive trousers. Certain distinctions in dress marked different classes—no buttons on cuffs for freshmen; buttons on cuffs for sophomores; ornamental coat fastening for juniors, except on cuffs; and ornamental fastenings on the cuffs for seniors. (Apparently, students loathed these class distinction markings and they were eventually abandoned.) On July 16, 1787, John Quincy Adams graduated from Harvard as a member of the newly founded chapter of Phi Beta Kappa.

and studying. John helped his son translate some works of the Roman author Cicero. Johnny also read *Don Quixote*. John wrote Abigail that their son was growing in body and mind and was known for "his general knowledge, which for his age is uncommon." His knowledge was practical as well. While waiting in port, Johnny was befriended by some sailors who taught him to swim, a sport he practiced for the rest of his life.

Finally on June 17, 1779, John Quincy boarded *La Sensible* with his father, and they began a six-week journey back across the Atlantic. This return trip was more pleasant than their rough sail the year before, and it wasn't long before Johnny was helping the French ambassador with his English. *La Sensible* reached Massachusetts on July 31, and Johnny and his father were warmly greeted by Abigail and the children. John Quincy was looking forward to entering an American school and starting his preparation for Harvard.

After only three months at home, John Adams was asked by Congress to return to Paris. John decided to take nine-year-old Charles and let Johnny attend a

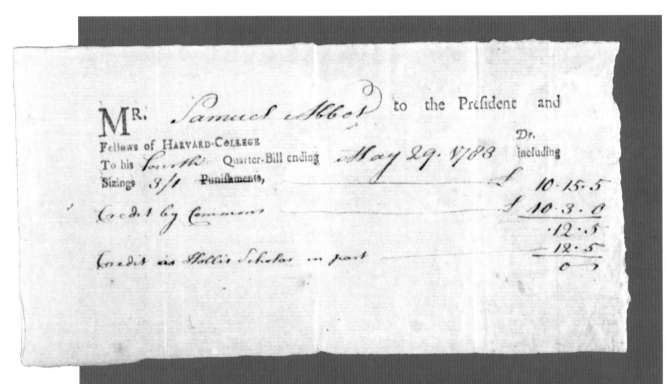

This May 29, 1783, fourth-quarter tuition bill for Samuel Abbot included a charge for "sizings," or extra expenses. For example, meat was served at dinner but jelly, ale, beer, and other items cost extra. These costs were called sizings.

Abbot also received financial credit for being a Hollis scholar. Thomas Hollis (1659–1731), a London merchant, was an outstanding benefactor of Harvard College. He endowed the Hollis Professor of Divinity as well as scholarship funds for poorer students.

Sums here are in the British form of pounds, shillings, and pence. This currency system continued to be used in the newly formed United States until the Coinage Act of 1792 instituted dollars and cents.

regular school. However, Abigail thought a European education would be better for her oldest son, and so both Johnny and Charles boarded the ship on November 13, 1779, with their father.

After they arrived in France, they spent some time in French cities, enjoying their culture. Finally, John, Johnny, and Charles reached Paris on February 9, 1780. Almost immediately, the two boys were placed in an academy in Passy run by the Pechigny family. John Quincy returned to the study of Latin and also had classes in Greek, geography, mathematics, drawing, and writing. He was overwhelmed by all his subjects and asked his father's advice on what he should concentrate. Adams advised him to give his attention to Latin and Greek and to develop his penmanship.

Just as John Quincy had settled into the academy and was enjoying translating some French fables into English, his father decided to make another move. Adams felt the French were hindering his attempts to make peace with the British. He made plans to leave for Holland and seek their support for American independence. John Adams and his sons left for France on July 27, 1780, just after Johnny turned thirteen. During August, as the family traveled through Holland, John Quincy studied Dutch, attempting to prepare himself for school in yet another country.

On September 30, the two boys were placed in a famous Latin school in Amsterdam, which had been established in 1342. Johnny hated it. The head of the school disliked the fact that Johnny couldn't speak Dutch and put him in an elementary grade. That humiliated Johnny and he became rebellious. John Adams quickly took the boys out of the Latin school and made arrangements for two private tutors to teach his sons.

John Thaxter had come to Europe as John's secretary, so he became one of the tutors. The other tutor was Benjamin Waterhouse, from Massachusetts, who was studying medicine at the University of Leyden. Johnny and Charles lived at Waterhouse's home while their father worked and lived at The Hague, the center of the Dutch government. At the age of thirteen, Johnny became an independent student at the university, which at the time was probably the best school in Europe. He took lessons from his tutors and attended lectures at the university.

Adams wrote from The Hague and told his oldest son to attend lectures in medicine, chemistry, and philosophy and to write him with full reports of what he was learning. John Quincy wrote back, "We went to hear a medicinal lecture by Professor Horn. We saw several experiments there. In the afternoon we went to hear a law lecture by Professor Pestel. Each lecture lasts an hour." Then he added, "I continue writing in Homer, the Greek grammar, and Greek testament every day."

By January 1781, Johnny was formally admitted to the University of Leyden. By that spring his father was concerned that his son was strong in Greek and Latin but ignoring his own language. He asked Johnny to begin reading English poets, telling him, "You will never be alone with a poet in your pocket." John Quincy not only read English poets, but he began writing poetry himself, a practice he kept up all his life.

In July, just after he turned fourteen, another radical change took place in Johnny's life. In later years he was convinced that this change damaged his education and continued the upheavals he had experienced since he was a small boy. Francis Dana, who had come to Europe as secretary to the peace commission that included John Adams, was sent to Russia by the American Congress. He needed a secretary who could speak French, the language of the Russian court in those days. John recommended his son because he was so fluent in French.

Dana and young Adams began their two-month, two thousand-mile trip across Europe. Though Johnny left his formal education behind, he learned much as he saw the differences between his own country and the small states he visited in modern-day Germany and Poland, as well as Russia. He felt that the rulers of these countries valued their animals more than their farmers. The two reached St. Petersburg at the end of August 1781 and were impressed by its beauty and size.

There was an immediate problem for Johnny however. There were no schools for him in St. Petersburg, and the few private tutors available were far too expensive. Johnny realized he would have to educate himself while there, and he began searching bookstores in the city and spending time in an English library. Johnny read all eight volumes of David Hume's *History of England*, and a five-volume work by Macauley, also called *The History of England*. He read Adam Smith's *The Wealth of Nations*, and Robertson's three-volume study *The History of Charles V*. He took up the study of German and became even better at French.

John Adams was pleased with his son's letters and realized that John Quincy was quite mature for his age. Adams was deeply concerned, however, that Johnny was not learning some of the basics of grammar and that he was not developing any friendships among Americans. The next year, when John Quincy told his father he wanted to return to Holland, John Adams gave him permission. Johnny left St. Petersburg on October 30, 1782, and set out for Stockholm, Sweden, the easiest winter route to Western Europe. On his own now, Johnny spent months traveling through Sweden, Denmark, and Germany and did not reach The Hague until April 21, 1783.

In Holland, John Quincy decided to continue studying independently with his father as his tutor. He read the New Testament in Greek, and, with his father's encouragement, read sermons as a way of relaxing. Johnny went with his father to Paris in August 1783 and attended the theatre again. He translated Caesar and Horace and copied English poets.

The American Revolution had officially ended with the signing of the Treaty of Paris in September 1783. After helping to negotiate this treaty, Adams traveled to England with his son in October 1783. In London, Johnny met two famous American painters, Benjamin West and John Singleton Copley. They introduced him to the finest artworks in the country.

Abigail and Nabby sailed for Europe in July of 1784 to meet Johnny in London. While he waited for them to arrive, John Quincy went to the House of

A page from the records of the Harvard Overseers meeting, October 13, 1785. At this meeting, the Harvard Overseers confirmed the appointment of Eliphalet Pearson, the first principal of Phillips Academy at Andover, as Hancock Professor of Hebrew and Oriental Languages. Pearson—called "the elephant" by students as a pun on his name and as a tribute to his bulk—was a dominant personality in the college for many years. John Quincy Adams was a student in Pearson's class during 1786–87.

Eliphalet Pearson kept an informal "Journal of Disorders." These are a few of his entries for 1788–89:

Dec 9, 1788. Disorders coming out of chapel. Also in the hall at breakfast the same morning. Bisket, tea cups, saucers, and a KNIFE thrown at the tutors. At evening prayers, the Lights were all extinguished by powder and lead, except 2 or 3. Upon this a general laugh among the juniors—

December 15. More disorders at my public lecture, than I ever knew before. The bible, cloth, candles, and branches, I found laid in confusion upon the seat of the desk. During lecture several pebbles were snapped, certain gutteral sounds were made on each side the chapel, beside some whistling.

December 16. Still greater disorders at Doctor Wigglesworth's public lecture. As he was passing up the alley, two vollies of stones, one from each side, were thrown at him.

February 24. Mackey was drunk in bed, and Dennie and Trapier were also highly intoxicated.

April 2. On Tuesday morning of this week, the Front door of Harvard was barred, the inner kitchen door tied to the buttery door, the chapel and hall doors braced too by a bench, the bell rope cut off, and the scuttle door fastened down by a board laid over it across the balcony.

The library at Harvard was the largest college library in the nation during the eighteenth century. It was located in the upper west rooms of Harvard Hall. The librarian had ten alcoves in which to arrange the books. Each Harvard librarian had his own book arrangement system.

The above is the charging list for James Bowdoin, 1786–88. Bowdoin's political career began in 1753 when he was elected to the Massachusetts General Court, and his active role in state politics continued until the state ratified the Constitution thirty-five years later. In 1785, when he was elected governor of Massachusetts, he resigned as a Harvard Overseer as the governor was ex officio president of Harvard's senior governing board.

On November 14, 1787, the governor borrowed, signed for, and returned volume one of the Encyclopedia Britannica (second entry). Volume two was subsequently delivered to him. The Britannica is the oldest English language general encyclopedia. The first edition appeared in 1768. The second edition, which was published in Edinburgh between 1777 and 1784, was enlarged from three to ten volumes. This edition contained a new section of biographical articles and the expansion of the geographic chapters. It also updated the history sections. Bowdoin probably borrowed the second edition. No one knows exactly why the governor borrowed these volumes, but volume two does mention "James Bowdoin" several times. Eventually, the governor's son would donate the land and money to start Bowdoin College in honor of his father.

Commons to listen to debates among the leading politicians in England. When Abigail first saw Johnny after five years, she did not recognize him. At seventeen, he was fully grown. After their reunion, the entire family went to Paris and lived there for the next nine months. Johnny continued his Latin and math studies with his father's help and did some trigonometry and geometry. He also spent time with Thomas Jefferson, who was then U.S. minister to France, and with the Marquis de Lafayette, who had served in the American army during the Revolution.

When John Adams was appointed the U.S. minister to England in 1785, John Quincy had a difficult choice. He could stay on in Europe as his father's secretary, or he could return to the United States and go to Harvard. After seven years in Europe, enjoying the company of important intellectuals and artists, it was hard to think of submitting himself to a small college in New England with its rules and regulations. When John Quincy finally decided to return to America and begin the life of a college student, John Adams wrote the president of Harvard College to ask that John Quincy enter as an upperclassman.

Johnny sailed from France in May 1785, and arrived in Boston on July 17, right after his eighteenth birthday. Riding overland to Boston, he stopped in Hartford, Connecticut. He met poet John Trumbull who gave him a copy of his poem "M'Fingal." At the same time, Johnny bought a book, *The Conquest of Canaan*, by the Reverend Timothy Dwight, which he read with delight.

In August, Johnny met with Joseph Willard, the president of Harvard. Willard suggested that Johnny needed additional study in order to be admitted as an upperclassman. Johnny went to Haverhill, Massachusetts, in October to stay with his uncle, the Reverend John Shaw, who agreed to act as his tutor. Johnny studied ten hours a day, sleeping late and then going to his books late at night.

John Quincy describes some of his studies: "Immediately upon going to Mr. Shaw's I began upon the Greek Grammar…I then undertook the Greek Testament, in which I went before I came here as far as the Epistle to Titus.…I also finished Horace and the Andria of Terence. In Logic I was equal with the class and in Locke about 70 pages behind them, Guthrie's Geography I had also finished." His aunt wrote to Abigail that Johnny went after knowledge like it was food. On March 14, he hurried back to Cambridge, and, after an examination by Willard, three professors, and four tutors, he was admitted to Harvard as a junior.

Johnny followed the traditional classic education with an emphasis on public speaking. He was elected to Phi Beta Kappa, a society for persons who gain high scholastic honors. While a member he joined in on many debates. Johnny also joined the A.B. literary society and gave speeches on many subjects. He enjoyed math and science and particularly liked astronomy.

For the first time, Johnny made friends among his own countrymen and developed some close relationships. Both of his brothers were also at Harvard, and they spent time together in Cambridge, traveling back to Quincy together on holidays. However, Johnny didn't have much good to say about the faculty. He criticized almost every faculty member, including the president, and only seemed to enjoy his Latin professor, Mr. James, who according to Johnny "knew his subject."

The class of 1787 had its commencement exercise on July 21. The topic of Johnny's speech was "Upon the Importance and Necessity of Public Faith to the Well Being of Community" and he received his degree along with his fifty classmates. Johnny was ranked number two in his class. His speech that day was published in the *Boston Centinel* on July 21. Less than a month later, Johnny took a stagecoach to Newburyport, a coastal town in Massachusetts, to begin his study of law under the guidance of lawyer Theophilus Parsons.

Parsons expected the men under him to work eight hours a day in his office and then four hours at home. John Quincy took a room with a woman named Mrs. Leather; her house was just a block from Parsons's law office. He began his reading assignments with Sir Edward Coke's *Reports* and *Institutes* and continued on with Sir William Blackstone's *Commentaries on the Laws of England*. He reread and enjoyed much more the *History of England* by David Hume and Edward Gibbons's *The Decline and Fall of the Roman Empire*. One book he read on his own was *Confessions* by Jean-Jacques Rousseau, which he considered the most amazing book he had ever read.

This period was the lowest time of John Quincy Adams's life. He became severely depressed during his first year in Newburyport and returned home to Quincy for a holiday in the summer of 1788. His parents had returned from Europe and he spent time with them. When he returned to his legal studies in the fall, his condition was worsened. Unable to study, he returned to Quincy and stayed there until March of 1789.

When John Quincy resumed his studies in April, his spirits began to improve. He became involved in a more active social life, began writing poetry, and had his first romance. By the summer, Adams had shown great improvement, and he visited his parents in New York City where his father had become the first vice president of the United States. Later that year, when President Washington visited Newburyport, it was John Quincy who wrote the address honoring him.

In July of 1790, John Quincy Adams received his master's of arts degree from Harvard. At the age of twenty-three he opened a law office in Boston. Soon, though, he began a career in public service that continued to the very end of his life. He was appointed to be U.S. minister to the Netherlands by President Washington in 1794 and later served as minister to Prussia (a state in modern-day Germany). He was a Massachusetts state senator, a U.S. senator, minister to Russia, minister to Great Britain, and secretary of state before he ran for president in 1824. He served one term as president and finished his public career as a member of the House of Representatives, in which he served for seventeen years. His speeches in Congress earned him the nickname "Old Man Eloquent."

John Quincy Adams married Louisa Catherine Johnson on July 26, 1797. He had met her in France when she was four years old and he was twelve, and

Above is a list of books borrowed by Joseph Willard between March and August 1786. Willard was president of Harvard while John Quincy Adams was a student at the school, 1785–87.

Willard borrowed several volumes of the Encyclopedia Britannica (entries two, five, and six). He also borrowed three volumes of "Cookes Last Voyage" (fourth entry). This library entry refers to Captain James Cook, *Voyages Toward the South Pole and Round the World...in 1772, 1773, 1774 and 1775*. These three volumes were published in 1777, two years before Cook's death.

they met again as adults in London, where they married. The couple had three sons who lived to maturity.

John Quincy Adams died on February 23, 1848, at the age of eighty, two days after suffering a stroke on the floor of the House of Representatives. It was written about John Quincy Adams: "He was…esteemed for his fearless conscientiousness, his ardent patriotism, his vast and various acquirements, and his unfaltering devotion to human freedom." He never stopped learning, reading and writing almost until the day he died.

—Bill Thompson

Andrew Jackson
Chapter Seven

News traveled slowly through the backwoods country of the Carolinas. Printing presses were unheard of in such villages as Hillsboro, Salisbury, and Waxhaw, so when the news arrived, it usually came in the form of a newspaper toted by a traveler from Columbia, Charleston, or Savannah, or even one of the great northern cities, such as Philadelphia or New York.

Chances are the newspaper was several days or even weeks old, but that mattered little to the people of those tiny, cloistered colonial towns, hungry for information about the outside world. This was particularly true in the summer of 1776, as fervor rose for revolution, not only in Philadelphia, where delegates to the Continental Congress were debating independence, but also in places like Waxhaw, South Carolina, where patriotic feelings were vivid and loyalists knew they would not be welcome.

Sometime in the midsummer of 1776 a newspaper did arrive in Waxhaw, and soon talk traveled throughout town and into the neighboring farm fields that it contained news of a most important event. As was their custom, the people of Waxhaw gathered in the town center for a public reading of the newspaper. Most of them did not have the ability to read, so the responsibility to stand before the crowd and deliver the news, word by word, fell on one of the few qualified readers.

On many occasions, that job fell to Andy Jackson—then just nine years old but, nevertheless, the best reader in Waxhaw. Years later, Jackson would recall that special job in the town of his childhood, claiming he could "read a paper clear through without getting hoarse…or stopping to spell out the words." And so, on that late July day in 1776, Jackson stood before some thirty or forty residents of Waxhaw, and read, "When in the course of human events…."

It was, of course, the text of the Declaration of Independence that young Andrew Jackson had been called on to deliver to the people of Waxhaw. It is doubtful whether the tall, skinny, and squeaky-voiced youngster delivered Thomas Jefferson's words with the same passion or enthusiasm that they were delivered with when Colonel John Nixon first read them publicly in Philadelphia on July 8, 1776. Nonetheless, Andrew's oratory skills were probably good enough for the people of

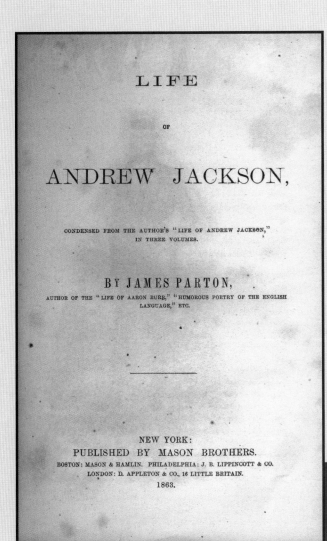

LIFE

OF

ANDREW JACKSON,

CONDENSED FROM THE AUTHOR'S "LIFE OF ANDREW JACKSON,"
IN THREE VOLUMES.

BY JAMES PARTON,

AUTHOR OF THE "LIFE OF AARON BURR," "HUMOROUS POETRY OF THE ENGLISH
LANGUAGE," ETC.

NEW YORK:
PUBLISHED BY MASON BROTHERS.
BOSTON: MASON & HAMLIN. PHILADELPHIA: J. B. LIPPINCOTT & CO.
LONDON: D. APPLETON & CO., 16 LITTLE BRITAIN.
1863.

ANDREW JACKSON.

Engraved by H. B. Hall from a painting by Earl

MASON BROTHERS N.Y.

James Parton (1822–91) ranks among the most successful writers of his generation. He also was Andrew Jackson's first major biographer. His three-volume *Life of Andrew Jackson* was first published in 1860, fifteen years after the President's death. Parton, who is referred to as the "father of modern biography," used primary written sources as well as interviews with people who had known the president. While Parton's conclusions are interpretive, he is praised for his historical methods. Subsequent Jackson biographers have built upon Parton's pioneering research work.

Parton wrote about Jackson's education: "He learned to read, to write, and cast accounts—little more. If he began, as he may have done, to learn by heart, in the old-fashioned way, the Latin grammar, he never acquired enough of it to leave any traces of classical knowledge in his mind or his writings....He was never a well-informed man. He never was addicted to books. He never learned to write the English language correctly, though he often wrote it eloquently and convincingly. He never learned to spell correctly, though he was a better speller than Frederic II, Marlborough, Napoleon, or Washington. Few men of his day, and no women, were correct spellers. And, indeed, we may say that all the most illustrious men have been bad spellers, except those who could not spell at all. The scrupulous exactness in that respect, which is now so common, was scarcely known three generations ago."

Waxhaw who, in just a few years, would make tremendous sacrifices for independence. And nobody in Waxhaw would sacrifice more than the Jacksons.

Andrew Jackson Jr. was born on March 15, 1767. His father Andrew and mother Elizabeth Hutchinson Jackson emigrated from Carrickfergus in Northern Ireland two years before Andy's birth. They made their way to Waxhaw, a tiny Presbyterian settlement a few miles below the North Carolina border near the Catawba River. Soon, the city of Charlotte would rise just to the north of Waxhaw.

Although they joined many family members in Waxhaw, no grant of prime agricultural land awaited the Jacksons when they arrived in South Carolina. Andrew and Elizabeth Jackson would become sharecroppers, forced to coax what few crops they could out of unforgiving red clay soil. In March 1767, a few days before the birth of his third son, Andrew Jackson Sr. injured himself while straining under the weight of a log. He died just a few hours later.

The man who would be elected seventh president of the United States was born to a widowed mother who was taken in by her sister, Jane Crawford, and her husband, James, earning her keep as a housekeeper and nurse for Jane, who was ill. In addition to Andy Jr., Elizabeth would raise her two older sons in the Crawford home—Hugh, three years old at the time of Andy's birth, and Robert, two years Andy's senior.

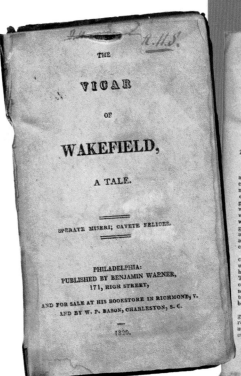

Robert V. Remini, the distinguished biographer of Andrew Jackson, writes, "It was also said—again unfairly—that the only secular book Jackson ever read from cover to cover was *The Vicar of Wakefield*. True, he prized the *Vicar* above all other books after the Bible, but the extent of the library he left upon his death raises doubts about his reading limitations."

Oliver Goldsmith's 1766 novel is the story of the Vicar's strength of character during times of great difficulty. Also, the book is a rejection of the ostentatious style of many novels of the time. Perhaps, Jackson identified both with the Vicar and with Goldsmith, who maintained his provincial manners in the midst of the sophisticated Londoners among whom he moved.

At left are the title and the opening pages from the second American edition of *The Vicar of Wakefield* (1820).

Elizabeth Jackson was not totally lacking in resources—family members in Northern Ireland, aware of the woman's plight, regularly sent her support, which is probably how Elizabeth was able to send her youngest and brightest child to school.

Andy started school at the age of five, attending what was known as an "old-field" school. In the rural South, old fields were fields that had been sapped of their rich soil by season after season of cotton, tobacco, and crop farming. As the fields were left fallow, pine trees would grow in place of the crops, eventually creating a dense, forested patch of land. In such old fields, it was not unusual for villagers to find a place for a school, clear away some pine trees, and erect a small building. Usually, the schools were built after an itinerant clergyman arrived in town and announced that he was qualified to teach school and would do so for a modest salary, as long as the villagers provided him with a school and, of course, pupils.

Students sat in rows on benches made from split logs. Long but thin wooden planks served as writing desks. Mud was slapped in the walls between the pine logs to keep the winter chill out and the warmth of the fireplace in, but the schools were damp and poorly lit.

Andy's first teacher in the old-field school of Waxhaw was Dr. William Humphries, who instructed his charges in reading, writing, and mathematics or, as it was more commonly known at the time, "casting accounts." Humphries was advised by the town fathers to teach the type of arithmetic a farm boy would need to know—how to count the coins paid by the miller for a bushel of corn, for example.

Books were scarce in Waxhaw and in his later years Andrew Jackson would never impress his contemporaries with his knowledge of literature. Nevertheless, as President Jackson would occasionally quote Shakespeare, it is obvious that he had read the Bard of Avon during his childhood. He also told people that as a boy, he read Oliver Goldsmith's *The Vicar of Wakefield*, a novel that may have served to inspire him to stand steadfast in his beliefs during times of great tragedy and turmoil in his personal life and political trials. He also read that most common of books found in the rural South, the Bible, although he did not become a deeply religious man until late in life.

As an adult, Jackson would often express an admiration for Sir William Wallace, the thirteenth-century Scottish hero who was executed after leading an uprising against the English. Wallace, Jackson said, was "the best model for a young man....We find in him the truly undaunted courage, always ready to brave any dangers, for the relief of his country or his friend." It is likely that Jackson learned about Wallace in Dr. Humphries' one-room schoolhouse.

While Jackson excelled as a reader, his lack of talent as a writer remains somewhat enigmatic. Well into his presidency, Jackson seemed the most challenged of writers, giving little thought in his official communications to grammar, spelling, or syntax. It was not unusual for Jackson to spell the same word four or five different ways on the same page. This may have been caused by his learning to write late in comparison to when he learned to read. Another theory, however, is that injuries he sustained as a young man, including a shattered shoulder and a bullet that remained in his chest for forty-five years, caused him so much pain when he moved his arm to write that he cared little how he spelled or wrote. As president, he turned over the drafts of speeches, essays, letters, and other communications to a team of secretaries, who would recopy his correspondence, making the appropriate edits. Yet, when he delivered his remarks through oration, Jackson was a most eloquent and electric speaker.

Outside of class, Jackson was a wild, unpredictable boy full of zest and mischief. He enjoyed playing practical jokes on his classmates, but didn't enjoy it as much when he was the butt of their humor. One time, some boys handed young Andy a gun loaded to the muzzle with gunpowder and dared him to fire it, knowing full well the blast would be too much for the skinny Jackson to shoulder standing up. Sure enough, the charge knocked Andy on his rump, but before any of his chums had the chance to make light of the situation, he was back on his feet and delivering this warning: "By God, if one of you laughs, I'll kill him." It is said that no one dared laugh.

Jackson could be a bully, but he also had a good heart and never picked on smaller boys. Instead, he was quick to protect young boys whenever he saw others pushing them around.

He also loved sports. Andrew never needed much encouragement to participate in a footrace, jumping contest, or wrestling match. He loved racing horses, too, and as an adult would become a fine horseman.

Years later, Dr. Cyrus L. Hunter, a physician from North Carolina, wrote that his father, the Reverend Humphrey Hunter, had attended school in Waxhaw with Andy Jackson. Here is how Cyrus Hunter described his father's school days with the future president:

> My father and Jackson, of the same Scotch-Irish stock, imbued with the same religious sentiments and reared under the same moral training, prosecuted their studies together with that cordiality of feeling which pertains to kindred souls. I have no recollection of my father narrating any remarkable passages of Jackson's boyhood. He spoke of his making commendable progress in his studies, or his ardent and rather quick temperament. The impression left upon my mind would lead me to say that he was an impulsive youth, ambitious, courageous and persevering in his undertakings.

At some point Andy withdrew from the old-field school and enrolled in a private academy taught by a Presbyterian minister, the Reverend James White Stephenson. Elizabeth Jackson had apparently decided that her youngest son should pursue a career in the ministry, and that desire was likely the reason for Andy's transfer. Events unfolding in Philadelphia in the summer of 1776 would cut short Andy's education and any future he might have pursued in the ministry. The country was at war, and in a few short years the horrors of war would reach Waxhaw and, in particular, the Jackson family.

Hugh Jackson was first to lose his life. Andy's oldest brother died in 1779 at the

Battle of Stono Ferry, helping to repel a British invasion. Hugh Jackson succumbed not to a gunshot or bayonet wound but to heat and exhaustion. He was sixteen years old.

Charleston and Savannah fell to the British in May 1780. British troops and loyalists swept through South Carolina, committing atrocities against the rebellious colonists. A force of three hundred British soldiers under the leadership of Lieutenant Colonel Banastre Tarleton arrived in Waxhaw, slaughtering one hundred and thirteen villagers and wounding another one hundred and fifty.

A regiment of South Carolina volunteers led by Colonel William Richardson Davie vowed to track down Tarleton. Many survivors of Waxhaw, anxious to avenge the massacre in their town, joined up. Two of them were Andrew and Robert Jackson, who were too young to fight. Still, they served the regiment as messengers and found themselves dodging gunfire at the Battle of Hanging Rock.

Following the battle, Andy and Robert returned to Waxhaw. While staying in the home of a cousin, they were discovered by a British officer, who had them arrested because they refused to shine his boots. The Jackson brothers both sustained stab wounds in the tangle with the officer. They were imprisoned in a crowded, filthy jail in the town of Camden, some forty miles from Waxhaw, where their wounds were left to fester. Elizabeth Jackson learned of their imprisonment, rode to Camden, and convinced the British authorities to release her two sons. Both boys caught smallpox in the jail; by the time she got them home through a driving rainstorm, they were both in a grave condition.

Robert died two days after returning to Waxhaw; Andy survived, but it would take Elizabeth a year to nurse her boy back to health. He would carry the scars of smallpox on his face throughout his life.

With the War of Independence drawing to a close, Elizabeth volunteered to nurse American prisoners held on ships in Charleston harbor. During this duty, she contracted cholera and died. Her final words to her son, as she left Waxhaw for Charleston, were, "Make friends by being honest and keep them by being steadfast." Andy was fifteen years old and now virtually on his own.

For a time he lived with an uncle, Joseph White, and found work as an apprentice in a saddler's shop. It was during this period that he met many young gentlemen who fled inland following the fall of Charleston. These young men were Andrew's age, and they introduced him to the world of drinking, gambling, and mischief making. When the British left Charleston in 1782 and his friends returned home, he went with them. He didn't last long in Charleston. A grandfather in Carrickfergus had left him a small inheritance, which he quickly lost gambling on cockfights and dice games.

He returned to Waxhaw penniless. With no other paths open to him, Jackson presented himself to the town fathers as qualified to teach school. He held the job for a year.

By 1784, he was on the move again. Coming to the conclusion that with a new country and new set of laws, there would be plenty of business available for a

THE

HISTORY

OF THE

LIFE AND ADVENTURES,

AND

HEROIC ACTIONS,

OF THE RENOWNED

SIR WILLIAM WALLACE,

GENERAL AND GOVERNOR OF SCOTLAND.

*Wherein the old obsolete words are rendered more intelligible, and
adapted to the understanding of such as have no leisure to
study the meaning and import of such phrases, without the help of a glossary.*

BY WILLIAM HAMILTON.

TO WHICH IS ANNEXED,

THE LIFE AND MARTIAL ACHIEVEMENTS

OF THAT VALIANT HERO,

ROBERT BRUCE,

KING OF SCOTLAND.

BY JOHN HARVEY.

EDINBURGH:
PRINTED FOR OGLE, ALLARDICE & THOMSON;
M. OGLE, GLASGOW; OGLES, DUNCAN, & COCHRAN, LONDON;
AND JOHNSTON & DEAS, DUBLIN.

1819.

THE

HISTORY

OF

SIR WILLIAM WALLACE.

BOOK I.

CHAP. I.

Of our ancestors, brave, true, ancient Scots,
Whose glorious scutcheons knew no bars, nor blots;
But blood untainted circled ev'ry vein,
And ev'ry thing ignoble did disdain;
Of such illustrious patriots and bold,
Who stoutly did maintain our rights of old,
Who their malicious, and invet'rate foes,
With sword in hand did gallantly oppose:
And in their own, and nation's just defence,
Did briskly check the frequent insolence
Of haughty neighbours, enemies profest,
Picts, Danes, and Saxons, Scotland's very pest;
Of such, I say, I'll brag and vaunt, so long
As I have pow'r to use my pen or tongue;
And sound their praises in such modern strain,
As suiteth best a Scot's poetic vein.
    First, here I honour, in particular,
Sir William Wallace, much renown'd in war;
Whose bold progenitors have long time stood,
Of honourable and true Scottish blood;
And in first rank of ancient barons go,
Old knights of Craigy, baronets also;
Which gallant race, to make my story brief,
Sir Thomas Wallace represents as chief.
So much for the brave Wallace father's side,
Nor will I here his mother's kindred hide:
She was a lady most complete and bright,
The daughter of that honourable knight
Sir Ronald Crawford, high sheriff of Air,
Who fondly doated on this charming fair.

"Despite his limitations, Jackson was neither ignorant nor illiterate," concludes Robert Remini, Jackson's biographer. "He was a man of genuine intellectual power, formidable in speech and writing, and later in life, an excellent conversationalist." Remini quotes Jackson's 1822 recommendation to his young ward to read the history of the Scottish chiefs. "Considering his background, this recommendation was hardly unexpected. He always regarded Sir William Wallace as 'the best model for a young man....we find in him the truly undaunted courage; always ready to brave any dangers, for the relief of his country or his friend.'" Perhaps, as Remini says, Jackson could have been writing about himself.

William Wallace (c. 1270–1305) is one of Scotland's greatest national heroes, leader of the Scottish resistance forces during the first years of the long, and ultimately successful, struggle to free Scotland from English rule. (Wallace was the subject of Mel Gibson's 1995 film *Braveheart*.) Most stories surrounding Wallace have been traced to a late fifteenth century poet, Henry the Minstrel. In 1721, William Hamilton of Gilbertfield rephrased the old obsolete words into more intelligible English. It is Hamilton's edition that Jackson quoted both in letters and conversation.

Illustrated above are the title and introduction pages from an 1819 edition of William Hamilton, *The History of the Life and Adventures, and Heroic Actions, of the Renowned Sir William Wallace.*

young man familiar with America's unique legal system, Andrew resolved to become a lawyer. But his limited finances made law school out of the question; however, Spruce McCay, an attorney in nearby Salisbury, North Carolina, had agreed to take him in as a clerk. Under McCay, Jackson would read law, copy McCay's pleadings, run errands, and sweep the office.

He spent two years under McCay and six months under another lawyer, John Stokes—a survivor of the Waxhaw massacre—and would learn enough law to be admitted to practice before the courts of North Carolina on September 26, 1787. Later, he would become one of the more than twenty lawyers, from John Adams to Bill Clinton, to occupy the White House. His legal credentials would always be rather thin, though, due in large measure to his fondness for dancing, wooing women, drinking, and gambling that would occupy his idle hours while under the tutelage of McCay and Stokes. Indeed, his nights in Salisbury were rarely devoted to studying Spruce McCay's law books.

There was a dancing school in Salisbury where Jackson became one of the most devoted of pupils. He was so fine a dancer, in fact, that the proprietors of the school asked him to organize the academy's annual Christmas cotillion, which was one of Salisbury's most important social functions. Jackson took on the responsibility with delight and saw to all the arrangements, including the delivery of invitations to Salisbury's eligible women. As a gag, Jackson also delivered invitations to Molly Wood and her daughter, Rachel, the town prostitutes. Jackson believed the two women would never show up, but when Molly and Rachel strode into the dance hall dressed in their Christmas finest, happily displaying their invitations, all dancing jolted to a halt as the fine members of Salisbury society gaped at the two prostitutes in astonishment. Molly and Rachel were soon shown the door, and Jackson was given a vicious tongue-lashing for his ill-advised attempt at humor.

Whether that event ruined his chances for a law career in Salisbury, or whether he always believed his future in law was best pursued plying his trade in the wilderness, Jackson elected to leave town soon after he had been admitted to the bar. Along with his friend and fellow McCay law clerk John McNairy, Jackson headed into the western Carolina wilderness to establish a practice. There wasn't much work for lawyers on the frontier, but in 1788 McNairy won an appointment as judge in a newly opened territory that included the stockaded village of Nashville. Jackson decided to accompany McNairy into the hill country, concluding that wherever a judge could be found, a lawyer was sure to find business. Jackson was able to establish a profitable law practice in Nashville, mostly as a debt collector, and was helped along by McNairy who appointed him prosecuting attorney for the town.

His appointment to the job by McNairy marked the first of many political connections Jackson would use for his own profit and to further his own career. He would make friends with a politically active attorney named William Blount, who was soon to be appointed governor of North Carolina. In 1791, his friendship with Blount resulted in an appointment to the post of judge-advocate for a county

For the rest of his life, Jackson quoted versions of his mother's last words

Andrew Jackson's mother died when he was fourteen. His father had died before Jackson's birth. His older brothers also had died. Jackson's biographers agree about his deep sadness. For the rest of his life, Jackson quoted versions of his mother's last words—words he said were the best educational advice that he ever received.

John Eaton, Jackson's earliest biographer and longtime friend, quoted him as repeating her famous last words this way: "One of the last injunctions given me by her was never to institute a suit for assault and battery, or for defamation; never to wound the feelings of others, nor suffer my own to be outraged; these were her words of admonition to me; I remember them well, and have never failed to respect them; my settled course throughout life has been to bear them in mind and never to insult or wantonly to assail the feelings of any one and yet many conceive me to be a most ferocious animal, insensitive to moral duty, and regardless of the laws both of God and man." (John Eaton, *The Life of Andrew Jackson, Major General in the Service of the United States*, 1817 edition.)

In a December 4, 1838 letter to Martin Van Buren, Jackson gave this version of his mother's advice—"to indict no man for assault and battery or sue him for slander."

Versions of the last words of Jackson's mother were well known in Tennessee. In 1907, a Nashville publication summarized her advice. Above is that summary from *Taylor-Trotwood Magazine* (May 1907, pp. 142–43). The author, John Trotwood Moore, had devoted himself to researching Jackson's life.

militia. Other than his brief service under fire at the Battle of Hanging Rock, it would be Jackson's first taste of military service.

When Tennessee was admitted as a state in 1796, Jackson served as a delegate to the convention that drafted the state's constitution. He later won his first election, going to Washington as Tennessee's lone member of the U.S. House of Representatives. Later, he would serve as a circuit court judge and establish a plantation outside Nashville. In 1802, another friend, Tennessee Governor Archibald Roane, appointed Jackson major-general of the Tennessee militia. In that role, he would in 1815 repulse the British invasion at the Battle of New Orleans, which established Andrew Jackson as a national hero and likely presidential candidate. Jackson chose not to challenge his friend James Monroe in 1816 or 1820. Instead, he waited until 1824 to run for president. He won the majority of the popular vote and more electoral votes that year than John Quincy Adams or Henry Clay but not enough to win the presidency under the terms of the U.S. Constitution. The election was thrown into the U.S. House, where Clay supported Adams, thus denying Jackson the presidency.

Jackson would, however, overwhelm Adams four years later. Most Americans felt a kinship with "Old Hickory," a nickname he earned because the soldiers who served under him believed him to be as tough as a hickory tree. After being elected in 1828, Jackson made the presidency into a truly powerful position, using the spoils system to hire and fire thousands of federal workers, guaranteeing that only those beholden to him would hold government jobs. He forged the modern Democratic Party from the remnants of the old Jeffersonian Democratic-Republican Party that had been divided following the 1824 electoral college fight with Adams and Clay. Jackson also expanded the nation's borders, often at the expense of Native Americans who were pushed off their lands, and by forcing Nicholas Biddle's Second Bank of the United States to make loans at low interest, which sparked a land boom in the West.

Jackson was, indeed, tough as hickory, a trait in his character that people who knew him as a young man found hard to accept. In 1860, Jackson's biographer James Parton searched through Salisbury for acquaintances who remembered Jackson as a law student. He found one elderly woman, who related to Parton her reaction upon hearing the news, some thirty-six years before, that Andrew Jackson was a serious and viable candidate for president of the United States:

> What! Jackson up for president? Jackson? Andrew Jackson? The Jackson that used to live in Salisbury? Why, when he was here, he was such a rake that my husband would not bring him into the house! It is true, he might have taken him out to the stable to weigh horses for a race, and might drink a glass of whiskey with him there. Well, if Andrew Jackson can be president, anybody can!
>
> —Hal Marcovitz

Martin Van Buren
Chapter Eight

In the late 1700s and early 1800s, the village tavern was more than just a place where a traveler could enjoy a tankard of ale while the coachman watered the horses. The tavern was a place where men of the village talked over the news, argued politics, convened town meetings, and even served as jurors and witnesses in cases involving petty infractions of the common law.

In Kinderhook, New York, a robust dialogue on the events of the day could usually be found at Abraham Van Buren's tavern. On the road between New York City and the state capital of Albany, Van Buren's tavern often served as a meeting place for some of the most important political figures of the day. It was not unusual for a farmer wandering into Van Buren's tavern for the purpose of quenching his thirst after a late harvest afternoon to find men such as John Jay, Alexander Hamilton, and Aaron Burr holding court and airing their opinions.

It is likely that Abraham's young son Martin helped keep tankards full while the men of the village talked over the disagreements between President John Adams and Vice President Thomas Jefferson, the XYZ Affair, the Reign of Terror in France, the growing abolitionist movement in America, or the ways in which the British continued to pose a threat to the United States nearly two decades after the War of Independence. Martin Van Buren was a bright boy, easily the best student at the local school, Kinderhook Academy, but young boys knew to keep their mouths shut when the men had important business to talk over. Still, the future president of the United States was like a sponge as a boy— he absorbed all he heard and formed his own opinions, particularly when it came to discussions of Thomas Jefferson's ideas about a minimalist government and the protection of human rights.

In Abraham Van Buren's tavern, the conversations were often conducted in Dutch. Dutch homesteaders had settled Kinderhook in the 1600s shortly after Henry Hudson sailed up the river that bears his name. Kinderhook, a Dutch word that means "Children's Corner," is located some five miles east of the river and about ten miles south of Albany.

Abraham Van Buren was a second-generation Dutch American who inherited the tavern in Kinderhook as well as an adjacent farm from his father.

Martin Van Buren was born December 5, 1782, in the family living quarters of the one-and-a-half-story clapboard tavern in Kinderhook. Born six years after the signing of the Declaration of Independence, Van Buren would become the first president not to have been a citizen of a country other than the United States.

Abraham Van Buren was a second-generation Dutch American who inherited the tavern in Kinderhook as well as an adjacent one hundred acre farm from his father. Abraham also inherited six slaves who worked on the farm and helped Martin's mother, Marie, in the tavern kitchen. Marie was a widow with three children when she married Abraham. They had five children of their own. Martin arrived third behind two older sisters and ahead of two younger brothers.

The Van Burens were not wealthy. Abraham Van Buren was a generous man and patrons of his tavern found him willing to extend credit or offer a loan. The fact that those loans were rarely paid back had much to do with the Van Buren family's modest circumstances. Still, they found the means to send their children to the local school. Kinderhook Academy was a run-down one-room schoolhouse in a hilly part of town. Little sunlight fell through the school's windows, which made reading difficult. The children were divided in rows not by class, but by age and size. Attendance was sporadic because the children were often needed in the fields. During the long winter months there were no crops to tend, but snowfall was often heavy and the young children found it difficult to trudge through the deep drifts. The teacher, David B. Warden, was dedicated and well educated himself, and the children of Kinderhook were well served by the school whenever they managed to attend.

Marie Van Buren insisted that her children keep up with their studies. Because little "Mat" was so bright, she was particularly keen on the boy pursuing his education. After all, Warden had raved to Mrs. Van Buren that her boy could read and write English better than any other student at the school—an impressive accomplishment, to be sure, because in most Kinderhook homes Dutch was spoken across the dinner table.

Martin had an aura that set him aside from the other Kinderhook students. He was a small and delicate boy with reddish-blond hair that hung to his shoulders. He had bright blue eyes that were fixed steadily on his lessons. What's more, he was a happy young man whose disposition made him a leader among his peers. His quick mind and poise gained him a measure of renown among the adults of Kinderhook, although it is likely that some of them were suspicious of this most

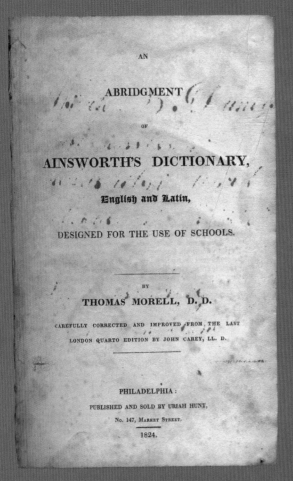

In his lengthy *Autobiography*, Martin Van Buren devotes less than one sentence to his schooling. Van Buren, the eighth president of the United States, learned Dutch as his first language. Descended from settlers who came to New Netherlands in 1631, his parents were frugal farmers and keepers of an inherited tavern who became respectable slave-owning citizens in the village of Kinderhook, near Albany, New York. Little is known about Van Buren's formal education. It is known that at the inadequate village school, he gained a fair knowledge of English and a smattering of Latin. We also know that his holography was almost illegible. After graduation at age fourteen, he became a clerk in the law office of a prominent local politician. It is here that Van Buren became fascinated with politics. He read little from law books but devoured almost every political pamphlet.

Latin, both as a spoken and literary language of the classical world, was a requirement in both public and private schools until the twentieth century. Above are pages from an 1824 edition of *Ainsworth's Dictionary, English and Latin, Designed for the Use of Schools.* First published in England in 1736, Ainsworth's *Dictionary* was a basic volume in almost every American school library through the mid-nineteenth century.

unusual young man. Years later, Van Buren wrote that Warden warned him about his "ardent, hasty, and impetuous" nature.

He studied Latin, grammar, rhetoric, and logic at the school. There were few books on the school shelves—the works of William Shakespeare were known to have been among them—but Martin had little interest in sonnets and plays, preferring instead to devour the Jeffersonian pamphlets he found on the tables in his father's tavern. In the tavern, the men talked about the rift between the Federalists and the anti-Federalists, who would soon become known as Democratic-Republicans (and eventually evolve into the modern Democratic Party). Over the years, Abraham Van Buren had found it bad business to take sides in political arguments. The tavern keeper maintained a staunch neutrality because he didn't want to lose customers of either persuasion. Nevertheless, Abraham soon found himself aligning with the Democratic-Republicans. His son, Martin, was turning into a Jefferson supporter as well.

In 1796, when Martin Van Buren was fourteen years old, he left Kinderhook Academy. It is likely that by that age, he had learned all that the village teacher was capable of teaching him, and few children would have continued in a village school past that age, anyway. The sons of farmers were needed in the fields. The sons of millers and tradesmen would have been expected to contribute their labor to the family welfare as well. Martin Van Buren, the son of a tavern keeper, would ordinarily have been expected to now devote himself full time to his father's business under the notion that, as the oldest son, he would one day inherit the tavern, just as Abraham Van Buren had inherited it from his father. The Van Burens, however, knew that their son was destined to be more than just a tavern keeper. James and John Van Alen, Marie Van Buren's two sons by her first husband, had become lawyers by working as apprentices to established attorneys. The Van Bureaus would have liked to send Martin to Columbia College in New York City, but their modest means made that impossible. Instead, Martin would receive his education in the law as his two half-brothers had found theirs. Francis Silvester, a busy Kinderhook lawyer and member of one of the town's most prominent families, agreed to take in the tavern keeper's boy as an apprentice.

Well into his adult years, even as he found himself a resident of the White House, Van Buren regretted his failure to obtain a formal education above what had been available to him at Kinderhook Academy. He felt that he had been forced to work harder to achieve his goals than men of lesser ability who were better educated. Van Buren wrote, "How often have I felt the necessity of a regular course of reading to enable me to maintain the reputation I had acquired and to sustain me in my conflicts with able and better educated men."

Nevertheless, for a man destined for a career as a master political intriguer, an apprenticeship under Francis Silvester was not a bad way to begin. By working for Silvester, Van Buren received more than just an education in the common law as it was practiced in Kinderhook. Silvester was also a close friend of the Van Ness family, wealthy Kinderhookers whose son William was pursuing a legal education himself at Columbia College. Martin benefited from this relationship, and Billy Van Ness and Martin Van Buren would later become very close friends.

Silvester was also an ardent Federalist, and he dressed the part. The dandified member of the bar was well tailored, spending no small amount of his income on stylish clothes and constantly admonishing his employees to always look their best. Van Buren, on the other hand, dressed like the son of a small-town tavern keeper. Although he took pains to keep a neat appearance, his coarse woolen clothes indicated his upbringing. This circumstance was rectified almost overnight. Several months after Martin joined Silvester's law firm, Francis's brother Cornelius, a Kinderhook storekeeper, spirited the boy away to Albany, where he outfitted young Martin in silken hose, silver buckles, and a suit of clothes that sparkled. From that day on, Van Buren had a tendency to overdress. (Some four decades later, that habit would cause problems during his presidential reelection campaign. In the campaign of 1840, the Whigs and their candidate, William Henry Harrison, mounted a vicious campaign against incumbent President Van Buren, accusing the president of being out of touch with the common people and pointing toward his ostentatious dress as proof of his snobbery. The smear campaign worked, resulting in Van Buren's ouster from the presidency. The fact that Harrison himself was a descendant of a prominent and wealthy family of Virginia planters must surely have been galling to the humble lad from Kinderhook.)

Van Buren was a busy employee of the Silvester law firm. In this era before photocopy machines, carbon paper, typewriters, or any other mechanized form of rendering words onto paper, Martin Van Buren's main job required him to copy, by hand, the long and elaborate pleadings that Francis Silvester would file in court on behalf of his clients. He also served writs and other papers and accompanied Silvester to court, toting the books and reams of papers his mentor would need for each case. Back in the office, he was also required to sweep up, dust the furniture, and keep the fireplace blazing.

Occasionally, Silvester permitted his apprentice the opportunity to take the lead in court. The courts of the era hardly resembled the solemn halls of justice found in county courthouses today. Taverns frequently served double-duty as courtrooms, and that's where Francis Silvester's caseload frequently led him, along with his eager apprentice.

In a tavern in the town of Valatic, not far from Kinderhook, Silvester had loaned out Van Buren to serve as an aide to Aaron Gardinier, a local attorney. The case was minor and the evidence was presented quickly. When it came time to voice closing arguments, Gardinier turned to his fifteen-year-old aide and said, "Here, Mat, sum up. You may as well begin early."

To face the jury, the diminutive Van Buren stood on a chair. History does not record whether Van Buren's courtroom oratory won the day for Gardinier's client;

nevertheless, the future president did report that Gardinier must have been satisfied with his performance because he paid him an extra fifty cents for the effort.

Van Buren's duties as a clerk in the Silvester law firm also required him to help out from time to time as a sort of night watchman in Cornelius Silvester's store, sleeping in the back room of the emporium on the clerk's night off. Like most people who had the pleasure of meeting Martin Van Buren, Cornelius had been impressed with the boy's intelligence and bearing, and foresaw a great future for his brother's apprentice. Cornelius was also aware that Van Buren regarded himself a Democratic-Republican. Cornelius was as much a Federalist as his brother, and he aimed to change the mind of the young apprentice. One night, while performing his overnight sentry duty on the cot in the rear of Cornelius's store, Van Buren found himself shaken awake by his employer's brother. It was well past midnight; nevertheless, Cornelius had selected that hour to win Van Buren over to the Federalist side. Later, Van Buren wrote:

> He placed himself by the [bed's] side, and for more than an hour
> occupied himself in presenting the reasons which ought to induce me to
> adopt the politics of the Federal party, and solicited me to do so with a
> degree of earnestness and obvious concern for my welfare which I could
> not but respect. After hearing him out, I replied calmly that I
> appreciated thoroughly the kindness of his feelings, and was well
> satisfied of the purity of his motives, but that my course had been
> settled after much reflection, and could not be changed. He paused a
> moment, and then took my hand and said he would never trouble me
> again on the subject, and would always remain my friend.

Van Buren remained with the Silvester law firm for six years. During that time, the rift between the Federalists and Democratic-Republicans continued to grow and become ever more vicious. In 1800, Jefferson defeated the Federalist John Adams for the presidency. Van Buren, long fascinated by politics, worked hard for the Jefferson campaign in Kinderhook. His labors so impressed Democratic-Republican leaders that they awarded him with a minor party post—delegate to a caucus meeting in Troy, New York, where his fellow Jeffersonian from Kinderhook, John P. Van Ness, was nominated for a seat in Congress.

Van Buren's activism on behalf of the Democratic-Republicans did not sit well with the Silvesters, although there is no evidence that either Francis or Cornelius sought retribution against the clerk. Still, Van Buren had worked for Francis Silvester for six years, and it is likely that by then he had learned all about the law that he was likely to learn as it was practiced in Kinderhook. In 1801, just before turning nineteen, he left Kinderhook to join his friend Billy Van Ness, the newly elected congressman's younger brother, as a clerk in a law practice in New York City. The departure from the Silvesters was without hard feelings on both sides.

When Van Buren arrived in New York, the city had not yet grown into the bustling East Coast metropolis it was destined to become. The wave of immigration that would cause New York's population to explode was still decades in the future. Still, in 1801 the population of New York was some 60,000 people, which made it one of the largest American cities of the day. If Van Buren believed that his clerkship under Billy Van Ness would lead to notoriety and wealth as an important big city barrister, he was mistaken. Van Ness had virtually no clients. Of course, as the son of a wealthy upstate family with considerable political connections—family friend Aaron Burr was now vice president—Van Ness always seemed to find a way to eke out an existence. For his part, Van Buren was forced to exist under far more humble circumstances. The two years he spent in New York were a time of poverty, missed meals, chilly nights in his rented room on Catherine Street, and lazy afternoons spent on New York's fashionable avenues watching the gentry stroll by. For a young man aiming to make his mark in the law, it was the worst of circumstances. For a young man whose first love was politics, however, Van Buren could not have asked for a better opportunity to learn about the intrigues of the city's powerful leaders.

At the time, the two most powerful families in New York were the Clintons and the Livingstons. De Witt Clinton was a member of the U.S. Senate and would soon become mayor of New York City. His uncle George was governor of New York State and destined to become vice president. Robert R. Livingston would serve as minister to France under Jefferson and negotiate the Louisiana Purchase. His brother Edward would serve a term as mayor of New York. What Van Buren found when he arrived in New York was internecine warfare breaking out between the leading Jeffersonian politicians in the city, with the Clintons and Livingstons on one side and Vice President Aaron Burr on the other.

One of the battlegrounds in this war was the political patronage system. With the Federalists ousted from power in the election of 1800, the Clintons and Livingstons swept Federalist workers from their city jobs and replaced them with committed Jeffersonians. Burr's allies received none of the jobs—all of the posts went to political workers who swore allegiance to the Clintons and Livingstons.

Burr struck back. He enlisted Billy Van Ness to write and publish a slanderous pamphlet under the pseudonym "Aristides" that attacked the Clintons and Livingstons as schemers who aimed to place their own man in the White House.

Both sides tangled for months, and both sides would suffer losses. Edward Livingston, serving as both mayor and United States attorney, would find himself engulfed in a scandal involving over $100,000 in missing federal funds. Livingston was forced to resign in shame and flee to Louisiana, where he performed penance by reforming the state's ancient Spanish and French laws. Burr was headed for trouble as well. His long-time feud with Alexander Hamilton ended on July 11, 1804, in Weehawken, New Jersey, when he killed Hamilton in a duel. Billy Van Ness, still devoted to the vice president, served as a second to

Burr on that misty morning in New Jersey. Later, a curious gambit staged by Burr to seize territory in the west resulted in his arrest on the charge of treason. He was acquitted, but his political career was over. Burr fled to Europe, returning to New York City in 1812 virtually penniless.

Van Buren's part in all these intrigues was no more than one would expect a poor law clerk to play—that of a fascinated observer who was fortunate enough to watch it all unfold from a ringside seat. In 1803, now overwhelmed by poverty, Martin Van Buren returned to Kinderhook to join his half-brother James Van Alen in a law practice. However, the two years he spent in New York City absorbing political lessons taught by such masters of the game as Billy Van Ness, De Witt Clinton, and Aaron Burr would serve him well years later when he joined forces with a scrappy ex-soldier named Andy Jackson to forge the modern Democratic Party.

—Hal Marcovitz

William Henry Harrison
Chapter Nine

When William Henry Harrison campaigned for president in 1840, his supporters in the Whig Party published a glowing biography of their candidate in which they extolled his humble "log cabin" lifestyle, as well as his military career as a fierce Indian fighter. A Baltimore newspaper soon picked up the story, reporting that the candidate's "table, instead of being covered with exciting wines, is well supplied with the best cider."

There is no question that Harrison made his mark as a military hero by putting down a Shawnee uprising at the Battle of Tippecanoe in 1811, but that business about hard cider and log cabins was stretching a point. True, Harrison had preserved an early settler's log cabin on his farm in Ohio, but he was by no means the type of man who could be found splitting rails down by the woodshed. He had been born into a wealthy and influential family in Virginia, the son of an aristocratic plantation owner and slaveholder who had signed the Declaration of Independence. America's ninth president studied for three years at Hampden-Sydney College in Virginia, where he absorbed the words of classical writers, finally ending his education in Philadelphia by spending a brief time as a medical student before turning to a career in the military.

Still, "Old Tippecanoe" did not discourage the voters from believing in his backwoods ways. His opponent in the 1840 election was the incumbent president, Martin Van Buren, who spent the campaign fending off the Whig allegation that he was a snob who dined on silver plates—an unfair charge inasmuch as Van Buren was the son of a New York tavern owner, born into far more humble circumstances than William Henry Harrison. The Whig Party would not exist much longer—it ran its last presidential candidate in 1852—but it made a considerable contribution to the American electoral system that is still very much felt today: the Whigs were the first political "spin doctors."

William Henry Harrison was born February 9, 1773, in Charles City County, Virginia. He was the seventh and youngest child of Benjamin Harrison V, whose family had arrived in Virginia in 1633, just twenty-five years after the founding of

William Henry Harrison entered Hampden-Sydney College, Virginia, in 1787 when he was fourteen years old. The college records for this period have either been lost or destroyed. Nevertheless, a most interesting document survives—the account book of Dr. Joseph Mettauer, a local physician. From Mettauer's page for "Will Harrison," (above) we can conclude that Harrison suffered an extended illness in August and September 1789. Mettauer was meticulous in listing the residence of his patients. The word "College" at the top of the page indicates that Harrison lived at Hampden-Sydney rather than at a local boarding house. Dr. Mettauer had come to America as the surgeon for the 5,000 French troops that arrived in 1780 led by the Comte de Rochambeau. Subsequently, he settled in Prince Edward County where he built up an extensive medical practice.

William Henry Harrison attended the University of Pennsylvania Medical School in 1790–91. He is the only president of the United States to have been a medical student.

Established in 1765, the Pennsylvania Medical School was the first such school in America. John Morgan, a native of Philadelphia and the school's founder, had studied medicine in London and Edinburgh. In 1775, the Continental Congress appointed Morgan "director-general of hospitals and physician-in-chief" of the American army.

This page from the *Minutes of the Medical Faculty* lists medical degrees conferred in 1790. In addition to completing the necessary course of study, each degree candidate had to write a thesis and defend it before the medical faculty. For example, Joseph Pennington of Philadelphia gave a satisfactory explanation of his paper on "the Phenomena, causes and Effects of Fumintation" (rage, fury, or agitation). Several medical students chose to write their theses and defend them in Latin.

The online version of the *Guide to the Archives' General Collection of the University of Pennsylvania, 1740–1820*, is an outstanding source for studying higher education during the era of the American Revolution through primary documents.

the Jamestown colony. William's mother, Elizabeth Bassett Harrison, was old-time Virginia as well; she was distantly related to the family of George Washington. By the time William Henry was born, the Harrisons owned plantations, mills, and a shipyard, and resided at Berkeley, a grand estate extending for miles along both shores of the James River. George Washington and Patrick Henry were frequent guests at Berkeley. Benjamin's distant cousin and close family friend was Richard Henry Lee, the delegate to the Continental Congress in Philadelphia who made the formal motion for American independence on June 7, 1776. A nearby neighbor, but hardly a friend, was a man named John Tyler. For years, Tyler would prove to be a constant political irritation to Benjamin Harrison; in an ironic twist, his son would later serve as William Henry Harrison's vice president and successor.

Benjamin Harrison served as a delegate to the Continental Congress and as governor of Virginia. He was a slaveholder who vigorously disagreed with abolitionist views. As William Henry grew older, he would come to oppose slavery and, much to the embarrassment of his family, join an abolitionist society.

Tutors who lived on the Berkeley estate provided William Henry's early education. In 1781 Berkeley was burned during the waning days of the American Revolution and the Harrisons decided it was best to send their young children away for the duration of the war. William Henry was packed off to Lower Brandon, an estate in Prince George County owned by Benjamin's cousin Nathaniel Harrison. At Lower Brandon, William Henry attended classes at Brandon School, a private academy established on the estate grounds by Nathaniel. By the time he was fourteen, William Henry was well-versed in mathematics and reading. It is also likely that he received considerable instruction in Latin and Greek, which would have been typical for a child of his background during the eighteenth century.

He may also have impressed his tutors with his interest in the natural sciences, because when it came time to pick a college for William Henry, the decision was made to send him to Hampden-Sydney rather than to the College of William and Mary, where George Washington, Thomas Jefferson, and James Monroe had studied. In Harrison's time William and Mary was the preeminent college in Virginia and the South. The Reverend James Blair, a relative of the Harrison family, had been one of the founders of the school, and at the time William Henry was to begin formal schooling his older brother, Carter Bassett Harrison, was studying law at William and Mary.

Although Hampden-Sydney had only been in existence for four years when William Henry Harrison began school, it had already earned a reputation as an important training academy for future doctors. This designation was owed mostly to the residency at the school of Dr. Joseph Mettauer, a prominent Virginia physician. One of Mettauer's students was James A. Jones, who would go on to become surgeon-general of the U.S. Army.

The school would grow in reputation as a fine center of learning. Although no other future presidents attended Hampden-Sydney, among the school's earliest graduates were George Bibb, who would become a U.S. senator and treasury secretary; Moses Waddell, who would go on to found the University of Georgia; William Branch Giles, a future governor of Virginia; and Patrick Henry Shields, who helped establish the state of Indiana.

In 1787 William Henry Harrison left Berkeley for Prince Edward County to commence his formal education as a doctor. Initially, he took classes in Greek, Latin, and history. He was a good student, but hardly a scholar. His selection of reading material indicates that he may not have been as interested in medicine as his family might have believed. Instead, he fancied himself a student of history. He pored over Homer's *Iliad* and *Odyssey* and read Julius Caesar's *De Bello Gallico* and *De Bello Civili*. All those works describe the art of war in some fashion and, in Homer's case, the romantic adventure of war as well. The tale of Greek warriors participating in heroic battles far from friendly shores may have made quite an impression on young William Henry Harrison, who just a few years before had been packed off to safety by protective parents because he was too young to fight the Redcoats.

He was also a devoted reader of Cicero's *Orations*. Here, again, was plenty of fuel to feed a young mind that had thus far seen little of America beyond the tobacco fields of Berkeley. "Courage," Cicero wrote, "is considered the undertaking of dangers and the enduring of labors. Its parts are magnificence, confidence, patience, and perseverance. Magnificence is the thinking about and executing of great and lofty things with a certain large and splendid determination of spirit; confidence is that by which, in great and honorable things, the spirit places great confidence in itself with fixed hope; perseverance is a stable and permanent persistence in a well-considered calculation."

Harrison maintained a fondness for ancient Roman and Greek history. In his correspondence and speeches, he often referred to ways in which the leaders of those ancient realms responded to crises. "Alexander toiled and conquered to attain the applause of the Athenians," Harrison reminded Simón Bolívar in a letter to the Colombian leader in 1829 while serving as U.S. envoy to the South American country. In the letter, Harrison admonished Bolívar to maintain democratic principles in the face of a rebellion. His letter concluded, "Will you regard as nothing the opinions of [the United States] which has evinced its superiority…by having carried into actual practice a system of government, of which the wisest Athenians had but a glimpse of theory?"

Twelve years later, Harrison peppered his inaugural address with references to the Romans and Greeks. In a reference to Caesar's duplicitous friend Brutus, Harrison said, "It was the remark of a Roman consul in an early period of that celebrated Republic that a most striking contrast was observable in the conduct of candidates for offices of power and trust before and after obtaining them. They seldom carry out in the latter case the pledges and promises made in the former." Later, Harrison's friend and future secretary of state, Daniel Webster, claimed to have read the speech beforehand and edited out numerous other references to assorted Romans.

Harrison's inaugural address was, by the way, the longest on record—an ironic distinction inasmuch as Harrison's presidency was the shortest on record. The address included nearly 8,500 words and required some two hours to deliver. (By contrast, President George W. Bush spoke just over 1,600 words on the occasion of his inauguration one hundred and sixty years later.)

At Hampden-Sydney, philosophers Charles Rollin and Hugh Blair were also among Harrison's favorite authors. Both men wrote on the *belles lettres*—the use and study of language and rhetoric. Later, Harrison would boast that he had read through the pondering prose of Rollin—which filled some 3,000 pages—no fewer than three times by his seventeenth birthday.

At Hampden-Sydney, Harrison joined the Union Society, which had been founded by tutor David Wiley and thirteen students "for the promotion of literature and friendship." The society would soon accumulate an enormous library for the college. Otherwise, his residence at Hampden-Sydney is marked by two illnesses the subject of the thesis of the graduate, and his place of nativity, or last residence.

4th. That there be two terms for graduating in the university — the one in April, the other in September every year.

Resolved.' 1st. That each candidate for a degree in medicine be privately examined before the medical professors upon the different branches of medicine, and if approved of, that he be directed to compose a thesis upon a subject chosen for him, or consented to, by the professors, which thesis he shall defend publickly after, which, he shall be admitted to the degree of M.D.

2d. That this Thesis be published, or not, at the option of the graduate.

3d. That a new form of a Diploma be composed, and delivered to the graduates in medicine, in the English Language, which shall contain with the usual matters,

In these 1806 resolutions, the trustees of the University of Pennsylvania formally established a written thesis requirement for the M.D. degree. A "new form of Diploma" written in English rather than Latin was authorized. Also, two terms of attendance were required for graduation from medical school—"the one in April, the other in September."

The medical Faculty beg
leave to inform the Trustees
of the University, that the can
didates for medical Degrees are
ready for an examination. &
request them to appoint a
meeting of the Trustees and
Faculty for that purpose to
morrow afternoon at 4 oClock.

W Shippen jr
Dean of M. Fy

April 18. 1792

suffered while matriculating at the college. The nature of those maladies remains unclear more than two centuries later, but there was no question be was under the care of Dr. Mettauer, who billed him for services rendered.

Of his years at Hampden-Sydney, Harrison wrote, "Inferior to many of my Class as a Latin and Greek scholar, I was considered but inferior to one in the Belles Lettres information and particularly in History. I was acquainted with the accounts of all the battles described by ancient Authors from Homer to Julius Caesar…This partiality for History is discoverable in my letters and speeches which have occasionally been published."

In 1790, at the age of seventeen, Harrison suddenly left Hampden-Sydney, spending a year in the state capital of Richmond as an apprentice to Dr. Andrew Leipner. He did not obtain a degree from Hampden-Sydney. Harrison's quick departure from the school may have been attributed to a change in the college administration—the president resigned the year before over a disagreement with school trustee Patrick Henry. It may also have been for religious reasons—Harrison's Episcopalian family may have been alarmed at the growing population of Methodists on the Hampden-Sydney campus. Whatever the reason for the hasty departure, Harrison's instructors must have believed he was now ready to prepare for a career in medicine, for without their endorsements it is unlikely that Dr. Leipner would have taken him on as an apprentice.

As Dr. Leipner's helper, it is likely that the future president would have performed minor medical procedures—dressing wounds or preparing sulfur compounds used as disinfectants. It was during his year in Richmond that Harrison made a foray into a social issue when he joined the Humane Society, an abolitionist organization of Methodists and Quakers headed by Robert Pleasants, a Virginia legislator long critical of Harrison's father for using slave labor. Once the governor found out about his son's zeal for social activism, the boy was recalled from Richmond and sent north to enroll in the medical department of the College of Philadelphia. Founded in 1765, it is the oldest medical school in America and today is the University of Pennsylvania's school of medicine.

In Philadelphia, Harrison was to be taken under the wings of two of his father's friends—Dr. Benjamin Rush and Robert Morris, both of whom had signed the Declaration of Independence. Rush was a professor at the medical school and staff physician at the nearby Pennsylvania Hospital, which was affiliated with the college. Morris, the financier of the American Revolution, was a prosperous Philadelphia banker. Harrison also found another familiar face on the medical school faculty: Dr. William Shippen, Richard Henry Lee's brother-in-law. Shippen, the first professor of obstetrics in America, was head of the school's department of anatomy, surgery, and midwifery.

Harrison arrived in Philadelphia in May 1791, taking most of his classes in Anatomical Hall on the campus of the College of Philadelphia. As a student under Rush, it is likely that Harrison would have learned the basics of anatomy and the techniques of healing as they were known then—doctors still bled their patients to rid them of disease in those days—but by the 1790s, Rush was also establishing himself as an authority on mental illness. (His 1812 book *Observations and Inquiries Upon the Diseases of the Mind* was the first psychiatric textbook published in the United States; it offered the groundbreaking opinion that insanity was a disease and not the result of demonic possession.) Still, in the 1790s not much was known about treating the mentally ill. Following his mentor around the corridors of Pennsylvania Hospital, Harrison may have seen the great surgeon's patients strapped into his "tranquilizer chair," a device invented by Rush to reduce the flow of the patient's blood to the brain. Rush's biographers have concluded that the uncomfortable device probably did no harm to anybody, but wasn't much help either.

Meanwhile, events were unfolding quickly that would prompt the future president to abandon his career as a physician after four months of formal training under Dr. Rush. Just after starting classes, he learned that his father had died. The aged revolutionary statesman had been ailing for some time.

William Henry Harrison inherited 3,000 acres from his father's estate, but found himself land rich and cash poor. The elder Harrison had made no plans to finance the boy's medical training—news that was delivered to William Henry in a letter written by an older brother. William Henry suddenly found himself without funds. By coincidence, Richard Henry Lee, then the governor of Virginia, was visiting Philadelphia. Harrison sought out his father's old friend for advice.

Lee suggested the military as a career. That summer, the Philadelphia newspapers reported many stories of threats by hostile Indians on America's western frontier. The idea obviously had great appeal to Harrison, who immediately left medical school and enlisted in the army. "In 24 hours from the first conception of changing my profession," Harrison later wrote, "I was an Ensign in the 1st U.S. Regiment of Infantry."

Morris found out about Harrison's decision and summoned the boy. Morris tried to talk him out of volunteering for the army, which at the time was undermanned and underfunded. In addition, Morris pointed out, life on the frontier facing hostile Indians was hardly the type of experience young Harrison had known in Virginia plantation society. However, Harrison was determined and Morris gave in, speculating that the western frontier was as good a place as any for a young man to embark on life's journey.

William Henry Harrison had a long and successful career as a soldier. He served as an aide-de-camp to General "Mad" Anthony Wayne at the Battle of Fallen Timbers in August 1794; this victory by the U.S. army opened Ohio to settlement. He rose steadily in the ranks, and was promoted to captain in 1797. The next year, Harrison resigned from the army to serve as secretary of the Northwest Territory, which encompassed the future states of Ohio and Indiana. After the Indiana Territory was separated from the Northwest Territory, Harrison served as governor for twelve years (1800–1812).

In 1811, Harrison became a national hero at the Battle of Tippecanoe when he put down an Indian uprising led by the chief Tecumseh, who organized a federation of tribes to repulse further settlement of Indian lands.

With the outbreak of the War of 1812, Harrison rejoined the army with the rank of brigadier general. He clashed again with Tecumseh at the Battle of the Thames in 1813. Harrison's troops defeated a combined force of British soldiers and Indian warriors. Tecumseh was killed in the battle, and his Indian followers scattered, never again to pose a threat to settlers in the Indiana Territory.

Following the war, Harrison and his wife, Anna Symmes Harrison, made their home on a farm in North Bend, Ohio, near Cincinnati. He was elected to the U.S. House of Representatives, but failed in a bid for the Senate. Later, he was sent as U.S. minister to Colombia, but was recalled by President Andrew Jackson after a series of diplomatic blunders. After returning to North Bend, the Harrisons suffered some economic misfortunes, and by the time the Whigs started their search for a

These pages list faculty salaries paid. (One John Matthias Kramer was discharged at mid-semester and paid half of his salary plus "a gratuity.") Also listed here are accounts with Peter Collinson and other London merchants for the purchase of medical books and medical instruments. Perhaps Collinson is best known for popularizing the writings of Carl Linnaeus, the noted Swedish botanist, whom Collinson met when the scientist lectured at Oxford in 1736.

The University of Pennsylvania agreed to pay for these ordered items with money raised from their next lottery. Throughout the eighteenth century, lotteries were used to obtain money for schools, churches, roads, bridges, canals, and other public projects. In 1748, funds obtained through a lottery were used to build Philadelphia's fortifications. And in 1826 a lottery was held to pay Thomas Jefferson's debts.

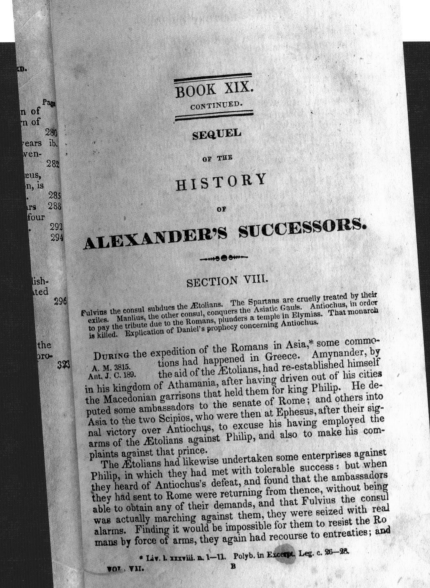

After his nomination for president by the Whigs in 1839, Harrison was asked to comment on his education. In his script, he wrote, "Inferior to many of my Class at College as a Latin & Greek scholar, I was considered but inferior to one in Belles Lettres information & particularly in History....I had actually read through the ponderous Work of Rollin which treats of Grecian & Roman history three times before I was 17 years old." Reference here is to French historian Charles Rollin's *Histoire Romaine dupuis la Foundation de Rome jusqu'a la Bataile d'Actium (Roman History from the Founding of Rome until the Battle of Actium)*, which was published in sixteen volumes between 1742 and 1751. An English translation was available when Harrison was a student. For decades, Rollin's histories of the ancient world remained popular in the United States. Voltaire described Rollins as "one of the first French historians who wrote a good style in prose."

Rollin's eight-volume *Ancient History* (1829) was used in American secondary schools and colleges until the early 20th century. Many editions and condensations exist. The chronology at the end of each volume is still considered the most extensive and detailed of the ancient world. Later writers on ancient history, such as James Henry Breasted, relied heavily on Rollin's pioneering volumes.

presidential candidate Harrison was working as a clerk in a minor government office in Hamilton County, Ohio.

By the start of the 1840 presidential campaign, Harrison was sixty-eight years old and ailing. The Whigs took great pains to cover up his infirmities. Whig newspapers described the general as someone of "elastic vigor" who spoke in "trumpet-like" tones. As the campaign wore on, he assured Daniel Webster, "My health is indeed better than it has been for many years."

The real truth came out a year later. He took the oath of office on March 4, 1841, and made his long inaugural speech on a blustery, damp day. For all his verbiage, Harrison disclosed little more than his intention to follow Congress's lead. Old Tippecanoe did show an eerie prescience by assuring the American people that he would not serve a second term. Shortly after his inauguration, President Harrison caught a cold that developed into pneumonia, and he died on April 4, 1841, after just a month in office.

—Hal Marcovitz

This is a record of student tuition fees and charges for firewood and quill pens collected by the University of Pennsylvania, 1768.

John Tyler
Chapter Ten

Nine-year-old John Tyler was a delicate boy who was regarded as rather docile. Most boys John Tyler's age enjoyed hunting and fishing with their fathers on their comfortable Virginia estates and plantations. Not young John. He preferred to spend his spare time playing his violin and writing poetry. Any suspicions that he was a pampered sissy, however, were instantly dispelled one day in 1800, when John was attending a school led by a Mr. McMurdo, a dictatorial Scottish schoolmaster who brooked no shenanigans from the sons of the wealthy plantation owners that had hired him to teach their children. McMurdo kept a birch switch on his desk and did not hesitate to use it at the slightest provocation. There is no evidence that John ever felt the sting of McMurdo's switch. Still, years later he noted, "It was a wonder that he did not whip all the sense out of his scholars."

The incident that touched off the uprising in McMurdo's schoolhouse remains unclear. Nevertheless, the students were moved to revolt against McMurdo's cruelty, and much to the astonishment of all who knew him the leader of the rebellion was the ordinarily docile violin player, John Tyler. Evidently, the students surrounded McMurdo, overpowered him, tied his hands and feet, and locked him in the schoolhouse. A passerby who heard the man's pleas for help rescued the hapless schoolmaster after several hours of imprisonment.

Once freed from his bonds, McMurdo went immediately to Greenway, the estate where John lived with his father, Judge John Tyler Sr. The indignant McMurdo related the events of the day to the judge, naming his son as the ringleader. The elder Tyler was unmoved by McMurdo's complaint. Clearly, the stories of McMurdo's despotism had made it to the judge's ears, and he had no sympathy for the Scotsman. He dismissed McMurdo with the words *sic semper tyrannis*—the Latin phrase that serves as the motto for the state of Virginia, which means "ever thus to tyrants!"

John Tyler, tenth president of the United States, was born on March 29, 1790. He was one of eight children of John and Mary Armistead Tyler. Greenway, the Tyler estate, covered some 1,200 acres along the James River near Charles City,

Nine-year-old John Tyler was a delicate boy who was regarded as rather docile.…He preferred to spend his spare time playing his violin and writing poetry.

The Sir Christopher Wren Building at the College of William and Mary is the oldest academic building in continuous use in the United States. It was constructed between 1695 and 1699, before Williamsburg was founded, when the capital of the Virginia colony was still located at Jamestown. The building was designed by Wren, the famed English architect, who also designed St. Paul's Cathedral in London. The Wren Building has been destroyed by fire three times, in 1705, 1859, and 1862. Each time the structure was rebuilt, and for more than three centuries it has been "the soul of the College." This daguerreotype was done in 1855 and is the oldest extant one of the college.

In 1802, at age twelve, John Tyler entered the secondary division of the College of William and Mary in Williamsburg, about thirty miles from Charles City. He boarded with his sister and brother-in-law. Tyler began his college-level studies in 1805 and graduated from the school with the class of 1807.

In this June 1807 letter to his classmate John Blow, Tyler described working on his senior oration.

Virginia. Charles City could be found about midway between Virginia's two great cities of the era, Williamsburg and Richmond.

The first Tyler to arrive in America was Henry Tyler, an Englishman who set foot in Virginia just forty-four years after the Jamestown colony was established in 1607. The Tylers would become wealthy and influential members of the Virginia planter aristocracy—a social class that produced George Washington, Thomas Jefferson, James Monroe, and James Madison, among others. The elder John Tyler fought in the American War for Independence alongside Patrick Henry. Following the war, he took up the practice of law and was soon appointed judge. He served in the Virginia legislature and later as governor. He also owned forty slaves and believed vehemently in the rights of states to determine their own destinies—an uncompromising philosophy his son would adopt as his own.

John's mother believed her son was destined for great accomplishments. It is said that on a moonlit night just a year after his birth, she saw her boy reaching skyward with his two chubby hands in a vain effort to grasp the moon. Astonished by what she saw, Mary Tyler is said to have remarked, "This child is destined to be a president of the United States, his wishes fly so high." Sadly, young John would barely get to know his mother. Mary Tyler died of a stroke when he was seven years old. John was often ill himself. He was a gaunt boy who endured stomach ailments, bouts of diarrhea, and frequent colds.

When John was twelve years old he enrolled in the preparatory school on the campus of the College of William and Mary in nearby Williamsburg. By the time he stepped onto the campus in 1802, the Tylers had long been associated with the school. His father and grandfather had both been students at William and Mary, and Judge Tyler would eventually serve on the Board of Visitors, the panel that oversaw the operation of the institution. In addition, two of John's aunts were married to William and Mary professors.

John lived off campus, boarding in the home of an older sister and her husband, a Judge James Semple, during the two years he spent in the preparatory school. After this he was accepted as a college student at William and Mary, the second-oldest college in the United States and the preeminent school for the sons of influential and wealthy Virginians. John Tyler's classmates included William Crittenden, who would serve under Tyler as attorney general; Winfield Scott, who would become an important military leader and a hero of the Mexican-American War; and Philip P. Barbour, who would be appointed to the U.S. Supreme Court by President Andrew Jackson.

By the time John started classes at William and Mary, more than a century after its founding in 1693, the school was still very selective in its choice of students. Enrollment was usually limited to no more than sixty students a year. Years after he left the White House, John returned to the Williamsburg campus to make a speech, noting at the time how selective the school had remained since he studied there. He said, "Of the number of sands upon the shore of time, she boasts not, but of those rare and precious gems, which have been garnered from their midst, and which shine and will shine forever on her illumined brow."

Despite its prestige, the college had been through a period of turmoil by the time John Tyler commenced his studies there. Thomas Jefferson, who had graduated from William and Mary in 1760, continued to exert considerable influence over the school long after he left the Williamsburg campus. In 1779, Jefferson served in the Virginia legislature and drafted a law titled "Bill for the More General Diffusion of Knowledge," which was intended to vastly change the William and Mary curriculum. Jefferson's legislation abolished William and Mary's divinity school and charged the college with adding courses in the arts and sciences to its curriculum. Jefferson's law also established new teaching positions at William and Mary, creating professorships in philosophy, medicine, languages, and legal studies. When John Tyler arrived at William and Mary just two decades later, the college was still wrestling with the mission Jefferson had laid. In 1804 the college's endowment was a paltry $130,000, and the Board of Visitors was finding it extraordinarily difficult to find the type of men whom Jefferson had envisioned teaching William and Mary students. The college's curriculum was still rather narrow during Tyler's matriculation; his courses were limited to mathematics, economics, and classic literature.

Still, he made the most of his opportunity. In economics class, Tyler was assigned to read *The Wealth of Nations*, the landmark treatise on economics by philosopher Adam Smith, who postulated that the government should provide only a minimum of influence over the economy, permitting businesses to grow on their own. Smith's theory became known as *laissez-faire*, or free trade. There is no question that Tyler was influenced by Smith's work. Later, while serving in Congress, he opposed tariffs—taxes assessed by the government on exports and imports. During his White House years, Tyler fought hard against establishment of a national bank, vetoing measures that would have established a government-controlled financial institution.

Among the other books John read in his William and Mary courses were David Hume's *History of England*, which provided important lessons to a future world leader on the pitfalls a powerful nation would do well to avoid, and the political satires of Tobias George Smollett, who lampooned England's society, culture, and military. John also had a taste for literature, perhaps stemming from his days as a young poet at Greenway. He enjoyed reading the works of such British men of letters as John Milton, Alexander Pope, Samuel Johnson, Oliver Goldsmith, Thomas Gray, and Joseph Addison. He was particularly fond of Addison, the essayist and poet whose writings appeared in the *Tatler* and the *Spectator*, liberal English political journals published by Sir Richard Steele. Addision was a staunch believer in the rights of men, constitutional government, and free trade. However, Addison was more than just a political commentator. He was a master storyteller who was regarded as an elegant craftsman of words. John wrote that Addision "is considered the best writer in the English language. He paints virtue in her most lovely colors, and makes each sensitive mind her lover and admirer."

John Tyler became fascinated with political economics as a student at the College of William and Mary. (Politics and economics had not yet been separated into separate subjects.) Adam Smith's recently published *An Inquiry into the Nature and Causes of the Wealth of Nations* was the text. Tyler committed Smith's arguments to memory. Tyler's subsequent speeches on the tariff and free trade delivered as a legislator and as president were drawn almost verbatim from this influential work. Indeed, Smith's persuasive arguments for government non-interference in the economy complemented Tyler's defense of states' rights.

In 1776, Adam Smith published his seminal *Wealth of Nations*. He criticized the older economic system of mercantilism, with its regulatory and monopolistic practices. Smith urged that certain "natural laws" of production and exchange be allowed to work. Thomas Malthus, David Ricardo, and the so-called Manchester School followed Smith. Their doctrine was dubbed (by its opponents) *laissez-faire*, and, in its elaborated form, is still called classical economics.

Basically, classical economics held that there is a world of economic relationships autonomous and separable from government and politics. The economic world, in this view, is regulated within itself by certain "natural laws," such as the law of supply and demand and the law of diminishing returns. All persons should follow their own enlightened self-interest; as each knows his own interest better than anyone else—and the sum total of individual interests will add-up to the general welfare and liberty of all (except slaves). Government should do as little as possible, confining itself to preserving life and property. Government must provide reasonable laws and reliable courts to assure the discharge of private contracts, debts, and other obligations. Likewise business, education, charity, and personal matters should be left to private initiative.

There must be no tariffs—free trade should reign everywhere because the economic system is worldwide, unaffected by political barriers or national differences. As for the worker, according to classical economists before about 1850, he should not expect to earn more than a bare minimum living. Adam Smith called this principle the "iron law of wages." If the worker received more than a subsistence wage, he only would "breed" more children who would eat up excess profits. If discontented, the worker should see the folly of changing the system. For this *is* the system, the natural system.

The classical economic liberalism espoused by Adam Smith and his followers emphasized the free, unencumbered marketplace as the most efficient, equitable, and salutary mechanism for the distribution of goods and services in society. John Tyler repeatedly used these arguments in the South's struggle against all other interpretations of the Constitution.

Above are pages from an 1818 American edition of Adam Smith, *An Inquiry into the Nature and Causes of the Wealth of Nations*. The first American edition was published about 1790.

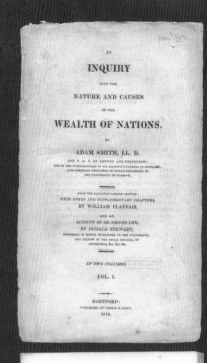

Tyler's favorite novelist, though, was the Englishman Edward Bulwer-Lytton, an unusual choice for a student so dedicated to fine writing. Although Bulwer-Lytton's novels are given credit for arousing the social consciousness of the British people, he is regarded by modern critics as a truly horrible wordsmith. It was Bulwer-Lytton who wrote the much-lampooned opening line "It was a dark and stormy night," which appears on the first page of his novel *Paul Clifford*. He was also the author of these familiar and well-worn words uttered by lawyers everywhere: "The pen is mightier than the sword."

Tyler particularly enjoyed Bulwer-Lytton's novel *Eugene Aram*. The novel told the fictionalized story of a real-life murderer hanged in 1759, yet portrayed as a hero by Bulwer-Lytton because of the man's intellectualism. John sat up one evening reading the novel until midnight, later writing that he found it "deeply and painfully interesting."

John received high grades at William and Mary in most subjects, but he had considerable trouble with penmanship. During his final year at William and Mary, Judge Tyler sent his son this rather strong rebuke: "I can't help telling you how much I am mortified to find no improvement in your handwriting, neither do you connect your lines straight, which makes your letters look so abominable. It is an easy thing to correct this fault, and unless you do so how can you be fit for law business of every description? Look at the handwriting of Mr. Jefferson, Wythe, Pendleton, Mercer, Nicolas, and all the old lawyers, and you will find how much care they took to write handsomely. Writing and cyphering well are absolutely necessary and cannot be dispensed with." There is evidence that John heeded his father's admonishments; historians who have examined John's presidential papers report that his handwriting was entirely legible.

John was a hard-working member of the student body at William and Mary and was well respected by his professors. Apparently, the hostility he had displayed toward McMurdo was an isolated incident in his young life, because he showed no such attitude toward his professors in Williamsburg. In fact, he was a favorite student of Bishop James Madison, the Episcopal clergyman who served as president of William and Mary, although there is one incident on campus that shows Bishop Madison was not always completely enamored with young Tyler. That incident occurred during commencement exercises in 1807. John was selected to deliver the commencement address in Bruton Parish Church in Williamsburg. Later, John wrote that his address was extremely well received by faculty members, who told him it was "the best commencement oration, both in style and matter, ever delivered at the institution within their recollection."

However, not everyone agreed. The topic for John's oration was whether more educational opportunities should be made available to women—a controversial topic at

> "I can't help telling you how much I am mortified to find no improvement in your handwriting," wrote Tyler's father.

that time. Evidently, Bishop Madison didn't agree with young John's proposals to permit women to participate in higher education. During the speech, Bishop Madison stood in the back of the church, gesticulating wildly with his hands and walking cane whenever John voiced an idea with which the bishop disagreed, apparently hoping that John would pick up the signals, drop the idea, and move on to another topic. Instead, John ignored the bishop and kept on talking. (It would be another twenty-six years before the first American woman would be admitted to a college in the United States.)

In the society into which John was born, it was common for sons to follow their fathers into the family's trade or craft. The sons of farmers became farmers, the sons of blacksmiths learned the ironworking craft, and the sons of brick masons became masons themselves. In John's case, his father had been a lawyer and legislator. That was the course John selected for himself. Following his graduation from William and Mary he intended to study law, writing that he believed the profession of law was the "high road to fame."

At the time, there were few law schools in America. Most young attorneys learned the craft of law by serving as apprentices or clerks to established lawyers. They would spend several years reading law books and performing menial tasks, such as copying lengthy pleadings, running errands, and even sweeping the office. In most cases, they would earn little or no money for these services, receiving their pay in the form of lessons in the law their employers provided for them as well as commitments to eventually sponsor them for admission before the bar of their state courts.

John's clerkship lasted two years. He started off by studying under his father, Judge John Tyler, as well as a cousin, Samuel Tyler. Within a few months, though, the judge was elected governor of Virginia, and he left Charles City for the state capital in Richmond. John went with his father, intending to continue his legal studies in the capital.

John served as an aide to his father. In 1809, former President Jefferson paid his respects to Governor Tyler in Richmond. Jefferson stayed for dinner, and young John made sure the great statesman had two desserts. When Jefferson saw the two servings of plum pudding placed in front of him, he asked the young man whether he was getting "extraordinary" treatment. "Yes," Tyler admitted, "but this is an extraordinary occasion."

When not helping his father, Tyler made friends in Richmond and joined a literary society, whose members met occasionally to debate social and political issues and practice their speaking techniques. Such groups were common on college campuses and in cities where men aspired to careers in the law and public office. After joining the society, Tyler became friendly with a young man named Abel P. Upshur, who would later serve under President Tyler as secretary of state.

Meanwhile, Tyler continued to study law. Because his father was serving as governor, he no longer had the time to devote to his son's legal training. Tyler began a clerkship under Richmond attorney Edmund Randolph, who had served as attorney general and secretary of state under President George Washington. Other attorneys in practice in Richmond during Tyler's clerkship included John Marshall, a chief justice of the Supreme Court, and William Wirt, soon to be President James Monroe's attorney general.

Tyler passed the bar examination at age nineteen. Under Virginia law, he was two years too young to practice law, but the examiner evidently never bothered to ask Tyler his age and he was admitted to the bar. It wasn't long before John Tyler had developed a thriving law practice. He gained a reputation as a brilliant criminal attorney with a dramatic speaking style. He was recognized as an articulate lawyer able to sway the emotions of many jurors into believing his clients were truly law-abiding citizens who had been falsely accused.

During this time in Richmond Tyler met Letitia Christian, daughter of a wealthy planter from New Kent County, Virginia. They married in 1813. By then, his political career was also off and running. In 1811, Tyler had been elected to a seat in the Virginia legislature representing Charles City. He briefly served with a company of volunteers, which had been raised to defend Richmond against British invasion during the War of 1812, but because the city was never threatened he saw no action during the conflict. After the war, he won election to the U.S. House of Representatives, served as governor of Virginia, and in 1833 was elected to the U.S. Senate. He had been a Democrat for much of that time, but split with his party and joined the Whigs, believing them to be defenders of states' rights, although he would eventually find himself incorrect in that assessment.

Meanwhile, an Army general named William Henry Harrison had become a national hero in 1811 when he put down an Indian uprising at the Battle of Tippecanoe. Harrison had been raised on a Virginia plantation not far from Greenway. In fact, Harrison's father, Benjamin Harrison, had been a long-time political foe of Judge John Tyler. The Harrison and Tyler families were never close, so it was truly ironic when the Whigs turned to Tyler in 1840 to serve as the vice presidential candidate on the ticket headed by General Harrison, who by then was living in Ohio.

The Whigs won the election for the aging general by portraying his opponent, the incumbent Martin Van Buren, as an elitist who was out of touch with the problems of common Americans. The so-called "hard cider and log cabin" campaign was highly effective—particularly for its motto, which remains one of the most familiar political slogans in American history, mainly for its alliteration and the jolly way it rolled off the tongue: "Tippecanoe and Tyler, too."

President Harrison would serve just one month in office. He caught pneumonia on the day of his inauguration and died shortly after. Tyler is said to have been shocked when he learned of the president's death—he had not even known Harrison was sick. One story that has circulated over the years reports that when officials arrived at Tyler's home to announce the death of the nation's chief executive, they found the vice president on his hands and knees playing marbles with his children. In any event, when Harrison became the first president to die in office, Tyler became the first vice president to ascend to the White House under the constitutional provision that provides for presidential succession.

Tyler would serve a single term in office, soon losing the support of the Whig Party. A true southerner, Tyler defended states' rights for his entire tenure in the White House. He would soon clash with the powerful Whig Senator Henry Clay, who believed in a strong national government. Clay supported the creation of a national bank, which Tyler opposed not only because of his devotion to *laissez-faire* economics but because he believed a national bank would impede the states in setting their own economic policies. Twice Clay pushed through legislation creating a national bank, and twice Tyler vetoed the legislation. In 1844, the Whigs refused to nominate Tyler for a second term, turning instead to Clay as their candidate. That fall, Clay was defeated for the presidency by James K. Polk.

After leaving the White House, Tyler retired to his Virginia estate. A believer in states' rights to the end, he supported the secession of the southern states in 1860–61. Soon after the outbreak of the Civil War, he was elected to a seat in the Confederate Congress. His service to the Confederacy would be brief. He died January 18, 1862.

—Hal Marcovitz

James K. Polk
Chapter Eleven

With his rural upbringing, young James K. Polk must have thought he had found a little piece of heaven when he arrived in Chapel Hill in January 1816. True, the North Carolina town was little more than a village consisting of just thirteen houses, two stores, and a tavern. A single muddy street ran through Chapel Hill, which the town fathers had somewhat optimistically named Grand Avenue. When Jim Polk followed Grand Avenue less than a quarter mile north out of Chapel Hill, he arrived at the campus of the University of North Carolina.

The school was just two decades old when Polk enrolled to commence his college education. Nevertheless, the college had grown quickly since it had been established as the first state university in the United States. By the time Polk arrived, the university was housed in three buildings. These buildings held classrooms and dormitories as well as a library, chapel, and meeting rooms where the school's two highly competitive student literary societies, the Dialectic and Philanthropic, held their meetings.

The university was located in some of the most beautiful terrain in North Carolina. The school's founders laid out the campus atop a ridge that offered the students a panoramic view of the forested North Carolina Piedmont. A student who gazed southeast through the cobalt blue Carolina sky could see smoke rising from the chimneys of Raleigh, the state capital, located some thirty miles away.

Polk had no trouble adjusting to university life. He soon became the top scholar on campus and a leader among his fellow students. Polk joined the Dialectic Society and took part in the group's lively and heated debates. In the 1800s, a college literary society was more than just a place where students could share their thoughts about books they read or recite essays or speeches they composed for the next day's class in rhetoric. The societies were also forums for political thought and social commentary.

In the early nineteenth century many college professors in America were also Protestant ministers or theologians, and had been raised and educated under strict moral codes that included a strong adherence to the lessons taught in the Bible. Few professors were willing to entertain radical thinking among students—even at North Carolina,

James K. Polk entered the University of North Carolina in 1815. The school consisted of a president, one professor, three tutors, and about eighty students. Nearby was the tiny community of Chapel Hill. Presbyterian instruction was the mainstay. Indeed, the president and the sole professor were Presbyterian ministers. Students attended chapel twice daily. On Sundays, black gowns were worn. Any student who questioned the existence of God was immediately expelled. After evening prayers, students were expected to return to their rooms to study. Tuition was ten dollars a term (later raised to fifteen dollars) and room was a dollar extra.

Polk was placed in the sophomore class, second half, because he did so well in the rigorous entrance examination that covered English grammar, Latin, and Greek. A classmate wrote that Polk "never missed a recitation nor omitted the punctilious performance of any duty." The future president, a timid person, formed a lifelong friendship at the university with John Y. Mason, who would later serve in Polk's cabinet, first as attorney general and then as secretary of the navy. Polk graduated in 1818, with first honors in mathematics and the classics. In June 1847 President Polk, accompanied by Mason, returned to Chapel Hill to attend graduation ceremonies.

These pages from the University of North Carolina Student Records and Faculty Reports, January 7, 1818, detail the academic examination of the university students conducted over several days in late 1817. Polk is listed in the twelve-member senior class that was examined on the Bible, moral and natural philosophy, rhetoric, and English grammar. The report concludes: "Distinctions might be made in scholarship, but it would be difficult at what point to stop. They are all approved."

These primary documents dealing with Polk's education are unique. They have been preserved in the archives of the University of North Carolina at Chapel Hill. Most southern college archives, as well as the schools themselves, were destroyed during the Civil War. In 1864, as General William T. Sherman's Union troops approached Chapel Hill, the university president rode out to meet him. He pleaded that the university buildings be spared. Sherman agreed but requested the use of the campus for his cavalry. Subsequently, the commander of the Union cavalry married the university president's daughter. This was truly scandalous at the time!

Each year, the entire University of North Carolina faculty tested the students. In late November 1816, Polk's fifteen-member junior class was examined in algebra, geometry, and English grammar. The final report noted, "In the class, James K. Polk, and William Moseley are the best scholars." Polk and Moseley, who later became governor of Florida, were roommates. In later years, the two friends reminisced about the "many tedious and laborious hours" they had spent in their room on the third floor of New College "attempting to discover the beauties of Cicero and Homer and the less interesting amusements of quadratic equations and conic sections."

"In the class, James K. Polk, and William Moseley are the best scholars."

where the senior year was totally devoted to philosophy, ostensibly to encourage the students to form their own ideas about how they planned to live the rest of their lives.

At North Carolina the college president, Reverend Robert Chapman, had modeled the school on the College of New Jersey (now Princeton University), a Presbyterian school. At North Carolina, Chapman insisted that prayer and Bible study be a part of the curriculum. The day commenced with solemn prayer in the school chapel. Prayers were said again just before supper. On Saturdays, students and faculty members were required to wear black robes and attend a public worship session.

While there were occasional tensions between Chapman and the students over the president's strict religious beliefs, there were political differences between the president and the student body. The Reverend Chapman was a devout member of the Federalist Party, which had dominated politics in the early years of the United States. However, by 1816 the Federalists were in decline and many Americans embraced the ideals of Thomas Jefferson's Republican Party. Nobody was more enthusiastic about the republican ideology than the young intellectuals on college campuses, who believed it was their destiny to lead the nation. The Reverend Chapman didn't see it that way, and he discouraged the espousal of Jeffersonian ideas on campus. By September 1816, relations between Chapman and the students were heading toward a confrontation. Clearly, some sort of student rebellion was in the air.

Jim Polk found himself caught up in the middle of it all. Even though he had been a student at North Carolina for just nine months, the other students were already impressed by his intelligence and poise and looked toward him for leadership. It must have surely angered Chapman when Polk, until then a faculty favorite, advised his fellow members of the Dialectic Society to stand up to the professors and speak their minds. "Stoop not from the true principles of honor to gain the favor of the faculty and thus succeed in your views of promotion," the future president of the United States told his fellow students.

Just a few years before making this statement, Jim Polk had not been the kind of erudite young man whose opinions were valued among members of the campus literary societies. He had grown up in rural Tennessee, and received a typical education for a boy whose family trade was farming—almost no formal schooling at all. After Polk made a name for himself in politics, his former neighbors recalled watching the president in his boyhood years skip barefoot down a dusty road, his pants rolled up to his knees and school books slung over a shoulder. That story may have been concocted by nineteenth-century Democratic Party managers eager to publicize Polk's humble beginnings; nevertheless, it cannot be denied that by the age of eighteen, the eleventh president of the United States could barely read and write. That was typical for a boy of Polk's backwoods upbringing, and if it were not for a childhood plagued by ill health it is likely he never would have set foot in Chapel Hill.

James Knox Polk was born November 2, 1795, in Mecklenburg County, North Carolina. His father was Sam Polk, whose Scotch-Irish ancestors had immigrated to America in the late 1600s. They settled in Maryland, but by the 1750s the Polks had decided to head south because they believed Maryland was getting too crowded for their liking. A year before Jim's birth, Sam Polk had married Jane Knox. She was the daughter of Captain James Knox, a wealthy Revolutionary War hero who died just weeks before his daughter's wedding. His estate left the couple well prepared for the hardships of life that awaited them.

Truth be told, though, the Polks would have fared quite nicely without Jane's inheritance. Sam's father was Ezekiel Polk, a wealthy North Carolina farmer whose talent as a surveyor led him to make some savvy investments in land. One of those investments was in middle Tennessee, some five hundred miles west of the Polk family's Mecklenburg homestead. In 1805, the land suddenly opened up to settlement—the Cherokees and Chickasaws having signed treaties giving up their rights to the territory. Years before, Ezekiel Polk had surveyed that territory and knew exactly where to stake his claim. Within months, Ezekiel Polk acquired thousands of acres near the Duck River in what would become known as Maury County. By the end of 1805 Ezekiel Polk had moved to Tennessee. A year later, enticed by Ezekiel's offer of several hundred acres of fertile bottomland, Sam and his brother William elected to leave Mecklenburg and start new lives in Tennessee as well. At the time Jim Polk, the oldest of Sam and Jane's five children, was eleven.

Sam and Jane Polk moved into a log cabin and began raising tobacco. The land was for the most part untamed and unsettled, and Ezekiel Polk found himself much in demand as a surveyor. Surveying expeditions into the Duck River wilderness often took days or weeks. Ezekiel would typically round up his two sons as well as his sons-in-law, cousins, nephews, and grandchildren and venture into the wilderness at the head of a large surveying party. Jim Polk was delighted to accompany the men on such missions, but he was a sickly, gaunt boy who tired easily. The boy was unable to keep up with the men—or even the other Polk boys his age. As a result, Jim would usually be left back in camp to tend to the horses while the others labored in the forests.

In addition to his lack of energy, as a child Jim often suffered from acute abdominal pains and raging fevers. Finally, his illness was diagnosed as a gallstone. Because doctors were not common in rural areas in 1812, the problem could not be cured until Sam Polk heard about a physician in Kentucky whose surgical skills were said to be remarkable. After a two hundred and thirty mile trip on horseback, Jim Polk went under the knife on Dr. Ephraim McDonald's operating table. Anesthesia was unknown in those days; the seventeen-year-old patient endured the incision with only brandy to dull the pain. He survived the operation, and after a period of convalescence returned to Maury County where he proudly showed off the small stone Dr. McDonald had cut out of his gut.

The surgery cured his abdominal pains, but Jim was still weak and unaccustomed to hard farm labor. Sam Polk proposed his boy learn the trade of a shopkeeper, and found Jim a job in a store in the nearby town of Columbia. The boy found the work not to his liking. Jim Polk had ambitions; clerking in a small town trading post was not

Literary societies provided important training at early American colleges. Students met periodically to debate public issues. Most students at Chapel Hill were members of either the Dialectic Society or its keen rival, the Philanthropic Society. Polk joined the former during his first term. Each society met once a week to debate a prearranged topic. Members were required to participate in these debates every other week and to present written compositions at the alternate meetings. The best essays were filed in the society archives. Eight of Polk's essays were so honored, and two of them still exist.

In Polk's first essay, "The Admission of Foreigners into Office in the United States," Polk worried about the deleterious influence immigrants might have on American society, including their possible formation of political factions and parties. Polk became a staunch Democrat but, in 1817, when the essay was written, many still considered political parties unnecessary. In the second essay, "The Powers of Invention," Polk expressed his strong faith in human progress through reason.

The Dialectic Society had libraries superior to that of the university itself. Polk donated many volumes, including John Eaton's 1817 biography of Andrew Jackson and a multi-volume set of Edward Gibbon's *Decline and Fall of the Roman Empire*. The Society strictly enforced its rules. Polk was occasionally fined for missing meetings and other infractions that included a ten cent fine for exchanging "threatening language" with another member.

Polk was an active member. He served as treasurer, secretary, and chairman of the executive committee. He also served two terms as society president—an unprecedented honor. The three pages above are from Polk's May 20, 1818, address to the Society thanking the members for electing him to a second term.

one of them. Now eighteen years old, Jim told his father he wanted to go to school.

Just south of Columbia, a congregation of Presbyterians had established a school in the Zion Church led by their minister, Robert Henderson. When Jim Polk enrolled in the school, he could barely make out the words on a printed page. Within a short time, Henderson had him reading the works of the classical Roman and Greek authors. Henderson was astounded by the pace at which this farm boy gulped down knowledge. After a year, Henderson told Sam Polk he had taught Jim all he was capable of teaching him. Young Jim Polk, Henderson said, "was diligent in his studies and his moral conduct was unexceptionable and exemplary."

Polk spent the next year at Bradley Academy, located some fifty miles northeast of Columbia in Murfreesboro, Tennessee. He studied under Samuel Black, a Presbyterian minister who led classes in Greek, Latin, mathematics, geography, philosophy, astronomy, the *belles-lettres*, logic, and literature. Classical Latin authors that Polk read at school included Lucian, whose dialogues were studied for their satirical content, and the historian Sallust, whose tales of the corruption of Rome and the deviousness of the traitor Catiline may have been used by Black to calibrate the moral compasses inside his students. Polk also tackled Julius Caesar's *De Bello Gallico* and *De Bello Civili*, which taught him something of the art of war, and studied the writings of the Roman poet Vergil, whose *Aeneid* tells the story of the wanderings of the warrior whose descendants would eventually found the city of Rome—important reading for a future commander in chief of an army that would later humble Mexico and seize its territory.

What's more, under Black Polk had cleansed himself of his farm boy ways and gained a certain academic polish, which may have helped him come to the attention of Sarah Childress, a wealthy Murfreesboro girl he met while attending Bradley Academy. The couple would marry in 1824.

After a year at Bradley Academy, Black declared Polk ready for college. Sam Polk, amazed at his son's progress, was anxious to see the boy continue his education. The choice of the college was simple—Sam's cousin, William Polk, served as a trustee for the University of North Carolina at Chapel Hill. The tuition was $10 a year, although during Jim's matriculation the fee was raised to $15.

Though Black and Henderson regarded him as the brightest of their students, few of their students had the intelligence or ambition for college, so Polk was nervous when he arrived in January 1816. He had to undergo a rigorous entrance examination—a committee of faculty members grilled him in his abilities to read English, Latin, and Greek—but Polk easily sailed through their questions. He did so well, in fact, that after a short consultation the faculty examiners concluded that his abilities already ranked him beyond the freshman level, and he was to be admitted as a member of the sophomore class.

He was one of about eighty students who would take classes at North Carolina that year. In addition to the dictatorial Reverend Chapman, the only

The above image is an 1813 paper cutout done of the University of North Carolina at Chapel Hill. The university was located on a great ridge from which one could look out across forested hills to see as far as Raleigh, the state capital, about thirty miles away. New College (later called South Building), the three-story structure on the right of the illustration, contained recreation rooms, the library, literary society meeting rooms, and the dormitory. Old East, the original two-story structure, is on the left of the illustration. The small village of Chapel Hill stood along a dusty road about three hundred yards from the university buildings.

other professor on campus at the time was Reverend Joseph Caldwell, who taught mathematics and philosophy. Tutors led most of the other classes.

Polk would not take his first class under Caldwell until his junior year. From that point on, he developed a close bond with Caldwell. Polk was an excellent math student, easily mastering the concepts of advanced geometry—no small feat for a boy whose prior exposure to mathematics had been limited to measuring out salt and sugar in the Columbia trading post. Caldwell also taught philosophy, which he had learned at the College of New Jersey under John Witherspoon, the sixth and most celebrated president of the university. Witherspoon had liberalized the curriculum at the College of New Jersey, adding lectures in eighteenth-century literature and rhetoric and placing more emphasis on the sciences. Witherspoon also subscribed to the theories of the English philosopher John Locke, whose defense of human rights and liberties may have had a lot to do with Witherspoon's participation in the Continental Congress and his decision to add his signature to the Declaration of Independence.

Witherspoon passed on those values to Caldwell, who in turn passed them on to Polk. Prior to enrolling at North Carolina, Polk had watched the rise of Jeffersonian political thought and the subsequent self-destruction of the Federalist Party. Back home, all the Polks, Jim included, were avid boosters of their fellow Tennessee citizen Andrew Jackson, who knew Sam Polk well. As a college student, Polk found himself focused on the growing national presence of the hero of the Battle of New Orleans.

The papers Polk wrote for class reflected the work of a budding eighteenth-century Democrat. One of his papers, titled "The Admission of Foreigners into Office in the United States," argued against permitting immigrants to hold elective office because Polk believed they would introduce an Old World monarchial government into what was then the world's only true democratic society. In the paper, he labeled the late Federalist Alexander Hamilton "a friend to aristocracy" and warned against "those who have been accustomed to cringe to the despots of Europe."

Most of his college papers were unabashedly patriotic. Polk believed wholeheartedly in the intellectual capabilities of Americans, and often pointed toward inventors and artists such as Benjamin Franklin, Benjamin West, and Robert Fulton to prove his point. He argued that only in a free democratic society could such "genius in rags" be permitted to blossom. By the time he left Chapel Hill, he had become an ardent Jeffersonian.

Caldwell was able to hone Polk's intelligence. Where Henderson and Black had merely opened the boy's eyes to knowledge, Caldwell taught Polk how to use his education. During his three years at North Carolina, Polk was twice elected president of the Dialectic Society—at the time an unprecedented achievement. He formed close friendships with students—his roommate, William D. Moseley, matched Polk in scholarship on campus and would later come close to nearly matching his friend's achievements in politics. Moseley would eventually serve as first governor of Florida.

Caldwell would take over as president of the college near the end of Polk's first year on campus and begin to do for North Carolina what Witherspoon had done for the College of New Jersey. For much of Polk's first year, however, the autocratic Reverend Chapman still reigned.

Events finally came to a boil one evening in September 1816 when Philanthropic member William B. Shepard defied Chapman's order to delete passages from his chapel oration. Angry words were exchanged and the chapel meeting broke up as students and faculty members shouted threats to one another. That night, the Chapel Hill dormitories were in tumult. The next morning, the Philanthropic members regrouped to plan their next move. They were thwarted by the faculty, though, which announced that anyone who would not sign a letter of recantation would be suspended.

That left everyone on campus quite unnerved. Even the members of the Dialectic Society, who had nothing to do with Shepard's rebellion, were upset by the situation. The Philanthropics accused the Dialectics of failing to come to their assistance, a charge that Polk refuted in strong language. Several of the Philanthropics refused to sign the letters of recantation; Chapman responded by suspending them. The ranks of the Philanthropics were soon down to just thirteen students.

When a bomb exploded on the doorstep of a tutor, the trustees of the college felt obliged to take action. Things did not go well for Chapman. Some of the trustees were fathers of young men enrolled at North Carolina; undoubtedly, they had been hearing complaints about the ill-humored autocrat for years. Chapman was ousted as president and Caldwell installed in his place. As for the students, they suffered losses as well. Shepard and another Philanthropic leader, George Dromgoole, were expelled. However, it would not be the last that Polk would see of either young man. Years later, Polk would serve alongside Shepard and Dromgoole in the U.S. House of Representatives—a legislative body that recognized Polk's leadership ability when it elected him speaker in 1835.

In May 1818, twelve college trustees arrived in Chapel Hill and spent a week interviewing members of the senior class. Polk astounded his inquisitors with the breadth of his knowledge. He was named top scholar and assigned the duty of delivering the salutatory address. Polk and the other graduating seniors reveled in the weeklong celebration on campus, which culminated in commencement exercises. Following graduation, Polk intended to pursue the practice of law, although he already knew his true ambition was to serve in public office.

In 1847, President James K. Polk visited the campus of the University of North Carolina to help dedicate a monument to Joseph Caldwell. As the students and faculty members of the now-thriving state university gathered before the president, Polk said, "It was here…that I spent near three years of my life. It was here that I received lessons of instructions to which I mainly attribute whatever success or advancement has attended me in subsequent life."

—Hal Marcovitz

Zachary Taylor
Chapter Twelve

When Zachary Taylor was twenty-three years old, he won a commission in the United States Army at the rank of lieutenant. Taylor considered his appointment to the military the fulfillment of a dream, and immediately sat down to compose a letter of thanks to Henry Dearborn, the secretary of war. Here is the text of young Taylor's letter:

> Sir
> I received your letter of the 4th of May in which you informed me that
> I was appointed a firs Lieutenant in the seventh regiment of Infantry in
> the service of the United States which appointment I doo accept.
> I am Sir with great respect
> your Obt. Servt.
> Zachary Taylor

Any high school or college English teacher would blanch at the composition, spelling, and grammar employed by Lieutenant Taylor in his correspondence with Secretary Dearborn. The truth is, however, that Zachary Taylor had no college English professor because he did not attend college. In fact, Taylor had barely any formal schooling to speak of. As a boy, he received just a brief education in tiny backwoods schoolhouses. By 1808, the year Zachary received his commission, he had long since devoted himself to tending the fields on the vast Taylor family property, where the nation's twelfth president learned the science of farming and, to a lesser degree, the art of war.

Nearly four decades later, Zachary Taylor found himself leading American soldiers in warfare against Mexico. By then, he had attained the rank of brigadier general and was, therefore, responsible for composing many letters and other communications to his superior officers as well as subordinates in the field. Some of those letters ran dozens of pages and contained explanations of complicated military maneuvers.

In one such letter, Taylor urged his superiors to authorize an invasion of Texas during the winter months, arguing that the climate of the rugged territory would be

Louisville Kentucky June the 6th 1808

Sir I received your letter of the 4th of May in which you informed me that I was appointed a firs Lieutenant in the seventh regiment of the Infantry in the service of the United States which appointment I doo accept.

I am Sir with great respect your obt servt &c

Zachary Taylor

The Honl. H. Dearborn S. at War.

In May 1808, Zachary Taylor was commissioned a first lieutenant in the United States Army. Congress had provided for a new regiment, the Seventh Infantry, and Kentucky's congressional delegation had recommended Taylor to the officer staff. Also, Secretary of State James Madison, a longtime family friend, interceded on behalf of the young man.

Above is the earliest known Taylor letter. It is addressed to the Secretary of War and was written on June 6, 1808. In it, Taylor accepted his army commission.

more favorable for the army's purposes than an advance in the summertime. Here is an excerpt from that letter, written on the eve of war with Mexico in 1845:

> On the hypothesis of an early adjustment of the boundary, and the consequent establishment of permanent frontier posts, I cannot urge too strongly upon the department the necessity of occupying those posts before the warm weather shall set in. A large amount of sickness is, I fear, to be apprehended, with every precaution that can be taken; but the information which I obtain leads me to believe that a summer movement would be attended with great expense of health and life. As in Florida, the winter is best for operations in Texas.
>
> I am, sir, very respectfully, your obedient servant,
> Z. Taylor.

No spelling errors. Complete sentences. Perfect grammar. Proper use of punctuation. Since winning his commission, had Zachary Taylor stayed up nights in his tent, reading spelling and grammar primers? No, the officer had no time for such pursuits. When not soldiering in the service of his country, he was home looking over his sprawling Louisiana plantation.

The difference between the two letters may be found in the fact that while Taylor certainly wrote his note of thanks to Secretary Dearborn, he may have simply dictated the correspondence regarding the inhospitable summertime climate of Texas, leaving it to a secretary to fix things up. Taylor's long-time aide-de-camp was Colonel William W. S. Bliss—a West Point graduate at the age of seventeen, speaker of six languages, and avid student of Kant and Goethe. He was also Taylor's son-in-law and, in all likelihood, the author of most letters and other communications that were issued under General Taylor's signature. Taylor said Bliss could be relied on for "trustworthy information, honest and competent advice, a friendly hand to supplement or subtract, and skillful pen to report, explain and, if necessary, discreetly color the facts." Zachary Taylor was so dependent on the colonel that he called him "Perfect Bliss."

Zachary Taylor was born on November 24, 1784, in Montebello, Virginia. Taylor would grow up to be president, but he would not join the ranks of the many presidents—among them Washington, Jefferson, Madison and Monroe—who would call Virginia home. Fact is, the Taylors were leaving Virginia for a new life in Kentucky when they stopped to visit a relative in Montebello just twelve miles from home. That is where Sarah Strother Taylor went into labor.

It can truthfully be said that Zachary Taylor was born in a log cabin. With no room in the main house to accommodate all visitors that day, the host family put the Taylors up in one of the outlying cabins ordinarily used by the field hands.

Taylor may have been born in a log cabin, but his family was far from poor. The first Taylors had migrated from England in the 1630s and settled in

Virginia just three decades after the founding of the Jamestown colony. By the time Zachary's father was born, the Taylors were wealthy and influential Virginia plantation owners. In fact, Zachary would share a great-grandfather with James Madison.

Zachary's father Richard graduated from William and Mary College in Virginia. He served in the War of Independence, seeing action under the command of General Washington at the Battle of Brandywine. He later served in the Virginia Assembly.

Richard Taylor was also a true pioneer. Before the war, he and his brother Hancock Taylor made their way south, examining territory that the American colonies obtained through Indian treaties. During the trip Richard procured some land five miles east of the tiny village of Louisville. On an autumn day in 1784, with his wife about to give birth to the third of their nine children, the Taylors set off to claim their property in Kentucky.

Following Zachary's birth, Sarah and the baby remained in Virginia for several months while Richard pushed on, anxious to begin the business of farming. In Kentucky, Richard established Hare Forest plantation, which eventually covered 10,000 acres in four Kentucky counties, making use of the labor of twenty-six slaves. In the beginning, though, the family lived in a log cabin Richard erected on the property along Beargrass Creek. In time, that cabin would be transformed into a magnificent mansion.

Richard Taylor was an educated and wealthy man who could have afforded to send his son to the finest schools in America. Sarah Taylor was well educated as well: as a member of the Virginia planter aristocracy, Sarah's lessons were taught by European tutors employed on the estate of the uncle who raised her. Zachary and his brothers and sisters, however, would receive just a small degree of the education their parents enjoyed.

Even for a family as well off as the Taylors, those early years in the Kentucky wilderness were rough and dangerous. Hostile Indians were said to be lurking behind every tree. Bears, wolves, and wildcats were also a concern. Recalled Thomas Cleland, Zachary Taylor's boyhood friend: "[Our] residence was on the edge of a dense cane-brake. Here we were saluted every night with the howling of wolves. In the meantime father had gone to look for his land. He was absent more than six weeks without our knowing the cause. The family was in painful suspense. The Taylor family, old and young, was very hospitable and kind to us. William, Hancock, and 'Little Zack,' as General Taylor was then called, were my playmates. Mrs. Taylor conceived a great fondness for my mother, and treated her as a sister."

An itinerant teacher named Elisha Ayers soon arrived in Beargrass country and was recruited by Richard Taylor to give lessons in the fundamentals of reading, writing, and mathematics to his children. Ayers was a Connecticut Yankee, but he was not a typical studious academic. He was a lanky, uncouth wanderer who traipsed from town to town in the backwoods South in search of work on the back

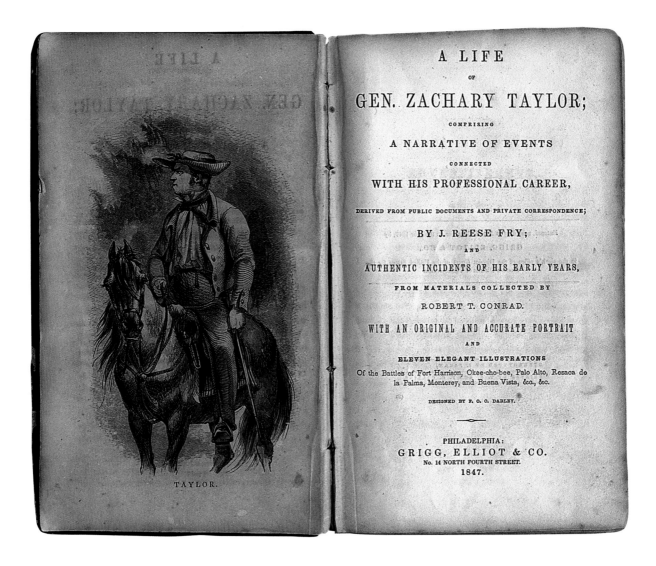

A LIFE
OF
GEN. ZACHARY TAYLOR;
COMPRISING
A NARRATIVE OF EVENTS
CONNECTED
WITH HIS PROFESSIONAL CAREER,
DERIVED FROM PUBLIC DOCUMENTS AND PRIVATE CORRESPONDENCE;
BY J. REESE FRY;
AND
AUTHENTIC INCIDENTS OF HIS EARLY YEARS,
FROM MATERIALS COLLECTED BY
ROBERT T. CONRAD.
WITH AN ORIGINAL AND ACCURATE PORTRAIT
AND
ELEVEN ELEGANT ILLUSTRATIONS
Of the Battles of Fort Harrison, Okee-cho-bee, Palo Alto, Resaca de
la Palma, Monterey, and Buena Vista, &c., &c.

DESIGNED BY F. O. C. DARLEY.

PHILADELPHIA:
GRIGG, ELLIOT & CO.
No. 14 NORTH FOURTH STREET.
1847.

TAYLOR.

of a mule. The Beargrass families built a schoolhouse for Ayers and enrolled their children. Ayers' specialty was mathematics.

Another teacher who provided much more practical guidance to the Beargrass children was Lewis Wetsel, a Kentucky mountain man who survived many tangles with hostile Indians. Wetsel is believed to have shown Zachary and his friends how to shoot straight—a skill to be valued in the Beargrass wilderness.

"The Kentuckians were then a warlike and chivalrous people and they were often engaged in offensive or defensive skirmishes with the Indians," Ayers recalled years later. "A number [of Indians] were known to be in the woods not far distant from the schoolhouse, and, on occasion, one of them was shot, wearing a British uniform. In their hostility to the Americans, they were encouraged and sustained by the British authorities on the northern frontier." There was a Mr. Wetsel in the neighborhood of the school, who, having been once chased by three or four Indians, loaded his rifle while running, and successively shot them all. This exploit made Wetsel famous, and he became the instructor of the young men and boys in his mode of maintaining a running fire. Among his pupils, it is believed, was young Zachary.

tinction increased. He received from President Washington a commission as collector of that port, New Orleans being then in possession of the Spaniards. He had been a personal friend of Washington, prior to his emigration from Virginia, and his worth was, therefore, familiar to that great man, from early knowledge as well as later report.

One of the chief cares of Colonel Taylor was the education of his children. During the first ten or fifteen years of his residence in Kentucky, the country being sparsely settled, and exposed to Indian enemies, this purpose could be accomplished only in a very partial degree. A school, for the rudiments of English merely, was established in his neighbourhood by Elisha Ayres, a native of Connecticut, who afterwards returned to that state, and now resides, a venerable gentleman of fourscore years, at Preston, in the vicinity of Norwich. A letter from him, written during the past summer to the author of this volume, in answer to one of inquiry concerning the school-boy days of General Taylor, explains satisfactorily the circumstances in which they were passed, and exhibits the character of our hero, at that time, in a light worthy of his mature reputation.

In the language of Mr. Ayres, "the Kentuckians were then a warlike and chivalrous people, and they were often engaged in offensive or defensive skirmishes with the Indians. A number were known to be in the woods not far distant from the school-house, and, on one occasion, one of them was shot, wearing a British uniform. In their hostility to the Americans, they were encouraged and sustained by the British authorities on the Northern frontier. There was a Mr. Whetsel, in the neighbourhood of the school, who, having been once chased by three or four Indians, loaded his rifle while running, and successively shot them all. This exploit made Whetsel famous, and he became the instructor of the young men and boys in the neighbourhood, in his mode of maintaining a running fire. Among his pupils, it is believed, was young Zachary." It may be remarked, upon this recital of "young Zachary's" first training in the art of war, that he has apparently forgotten

TAYLOR'S FIRST LESSON IN THE ART OF WAR.

The United States had found a new military hero after General Zachary Taylor defeated the Mexican forces of General Pedro de Ampudia at the Battle of Monterey (1846) and then the army of General Antonio López de Santa Anna at the Battle of Buena Vista (1847). City after city gave the general a hero's welcome. Immediately, several biographies were published. The one written by Robert T. Conrad is perhaps the best for studying Taylor's education. Conrad, a well-known Philadelphia lawyer and a history buff, went to Kentucky and interviewed people who had known Taylor as a young man. Conrad gave his notes to J. Reese Fry, an outstanding journalist, who completed the Taylor biography in 1847. Subsequent Taylor biographies have relied on the Conrad/Fry account of Taylor's education. The etching above, "Taylor's First Lessons in the Art of War," is based on those interviews and is the oldest known engraving of "young" Taylor. The pages reprinted here are from an 1847 copy of A *Life of Gen. Zachary Taylor* by Fry and Conrad.

Elisha Ayers recalled teaching Taylor. He said the future president was "quick in learning, and still patient in study." As for Ayers, wanderlust is said to have afflicted him, and in time the rumpled New Englander mounted his mule for adventures elsewhere in the Kentucky hills. His place in the education of Zachary Taylor was taken by Kean O'Hara, a much more dedicated and accomplished teacher. The hardy pioneers who chose to make their homes in the Kentucky of the early 1800s could hardly have expected to see someone in their midst whose academic credentials matched those of Kean O'Hara. A scholar of classic literature, O'Hara found himself on the losing side of the Irish Revolution of 1798 and was exiled from his country. Kentucky Governor Isaac Shelby invited him to teach in his state, which had entered the Union just six years before and was sorely in need of qualified teachers. O'Hara established a school in Danville near Lexington, and then moved to Louisville, where one of his pupils was Zachary Taylor.

Later, O'Hara's son, Theodore O'Hara, would become an important American poet. In fact, he would serve under General Zachary Taylor in Mexico and write an ode to the Kentucky boys who fell in the Battle of Buena Vista titled "The Bivouac of the Dead." The poem eloquently spoke about the sacrifices of war. Ironically, the Battle of Buena Vista was Taylor's greatest victory, and was primarily responsible for making the general into a national hero and likely presidential candidate. In June of 1848, just a year after the Battle of Buena Vista, the Whig senator from Kentucky, John J. Crittenden, gave a speech in his home state promoting the candidacy of Zachary Taylor for president. During that speech, Crittenden insisted that Taylor was well educated. He said:

> Not mere scholastic learning—he has never graduated at a college—but his mind is richly stored with that practical knowledge which is acquired from both men and books. He is a deeply read man, in all ancient and modern history, and in all matters relating to the practical duties of life, civil and military. He is intimate with Plutarch...a Plutarch hero himself, as bright as ever adorned the page of history.

Certainly, much of that robust rhetoric can be attributed to partisan boosterism by the Whig spin-doctors of the era. Yet, if what Crittenden said is true and Taylor did study Plutarch at least at some point in his life, it is not out of the question that the general was inspired in that pursuit by Kean O'Hara. And what would he have learned from Plutarch? A Kentucky farm boy dreaming of a career in the military would have been enthralled by Plutarch's recitations of the lives of the fifteen great Greek heroes, particularly the military leaders and conquerors Plutarch selected for his list. For example, Plutarch told the story of Philpoemen, the brave Greek general "who in actual fighting was as good as the youngest, and in judgment as good as the oldest, so that there came onto the field of battle no better soldier or commander." Plutarch also wrote of Pelopidas, who led the Thebans to victory over the superior Spartans. And Plutarch wrote of Alexander the Great, conqueror of cities at the age of sixteen:

> The neighboring states and the cities of Greece rebelled against Macedonian rule now that they saw a boy on the throne. Alexander's council advised him to give up trying to subjugate the Greeks and to concentrate on his own resources on keeping the barbarian nations of the north under control. Treat the Greeks kindly, they said, and that will dissipate the first impulses of rebellion. But Alexander rejected this advice. If any sign of weakness were perceived at the beginning of his government, everyone would be encouraged to attack, so only bravery was their safety.

Plutarch's writing about the glory of war could easily inspire any farm boy to long for the day when he could join the military.

Kean O'Hara's influence on Zachary Taylor was brief. The young man was needed in his father's fields. For the rest of his boyhood, Zachary would devote his energies to tending the Taylors' widening Kentucky plantation.

Away from the Taylor family's calm and bucolic fields, tensions continued to escalate between the United States and its old enemy, Great Britain. In 1806, Taylor briefly joined a regiment of Kentucky volunteers, hastily formed in response to Aaron Burr's apparently treasonous plot to grab for land in the West. Two years later, the opportunity finally arrived for Taylor to obtain a commission in the U.S. Army.

Sadly, he found the opportunity to apply for the rank through the death of his brother, William Taylor, who had already won a commission as a lieutenant in the Army's Seventh Infantry. In early 1808 William died while skirmishing with hostile Indians in Louisiana. Richard Taylor called on his influential friends in Kentucky politics to back his son Zachary for the vacancy. Letters were written on Zachary's behalf, and on May 3, 1808, Secretary of War Dearborn issued the commission for the young man to join the Seventh Infantry of the United States Army. For most of the next forty years, Zachary Taylor would be a soldier.

He spent the first few months of his enlistment helping to recruit infantrymen, then accompanied the Seventh Infantry to camp in New Orleans just in time to endure the hottest summer in years in Louisiana. The army selected the swampy region known as Terre Aux Boeufs to bivouac the Seventh Infantry, so many of the men, including Taylor, contracted yellow fever. Taylor was sent home to Kentucky to regain his health. It would be two years before he resumed his profession as a soldier.

When he did rejoin the Seventh, it was at the rank of captain. He had also taken a wife during his two years away from the military. Her name was

Margaret Mackall Smith, and she was the daughter of a prominent Jefferson County, Kentucky, family.

Taylor returned to active duty in time to serve in the War of 1812. Following the war, his career would take him to Wisconsin, Minnesota, Missouri, and Louisiana, usually to put down uprisings by Native American tribes. In 1837, his defeat of the Seminoles at Lake Okeechobee in Florida won him promotion to brigadier general. It was during the Seminole War that Taylor's troops dubbed their commander "Old Rough and Ready," in recognition of his iron constitution in leading them relentlessly through the murky Everglades as well as his fondness for plain uniforms.

His greatest victories, however, were yet to come. In 1846, he led 2,300 men in the Battle of Palo Alto against a Mexican army that outnumbered his men three to one. A year later, at Buena Vista, he again led his troops to victory against a much larger Mexican force. The conquest of the Mexican army at Buena Vista effectively ended the war, enabling the United States to annex Texas. Zachary Taylor was now a national hero.

Throughout his military career, Taylor continued to rely on Colonel Bliss. During the Mexican-American War, dictator Antonio López de Santa Anna sent a message to Taylor, warning the general that he would be "cut to pieces with your troops" unless he surrendered. Taylor is said to have reacted angrily and most threateningly, but Bliss stepped in and penned a diplomatic reply, declining Santa Anna's request with a curt yet smug message that the United States Army does not respond to hollow threats. "In reply to your note of this date summoning me to surrender my forces at discretion, I beg leave to say I decline acceding to your request," said the simple note, signed by General Taylor.

In 1848, the Whigs offered Taylor the nomination for the presidency. There were many well-spoken Whigs who often provided the appropriate words for Taylor whenever he needed them, such as Senator Crittenden, Representative Alexander Stephens of Georgia, and a young congressman from Illinois, Abraham Lincoln. In that era, it was highly unusual for candidates to take an active part in their campaigns. Bliss was on hand, as well; when his father-in-law was elected president, Bliss would accompany him into the White House as a trusted aide.

His inaugural speech was short—President Taylor uttered just over a thousand words, and left many of his Whig supporters wondering where he stood on the few issues he did manage to address. Sitting just to the side of Taylor during the speech was President James K. Polk, the man he replaced in the White House. Later, Polk told people that Taylor spoke "in a very low voice and very badly as to his pronunciation and manner."

Zachary Taylor's presidency would be short. Although a southerner and slaveholder himself, Taylor was against permitting slavery in any new state joining the union. It was during his brief administration that Senator Henry

Clay drafted the Great Compromise, permitting California to enter as a free state in exchange for adoption of the Fugitive Slave Act, which gave southerners the right to pursue runaway slaves in the North. Taylor opposed the compromise and threatened to veto the Fugitive Slave Act, but the bill never reached his desk. On July 4, 1850, after serving just sixteen months in office, he visited the Washington Monument, which was then under construction. It was a hot and muggy day in the nation's capital and Taylor suffered from the heat. That night, he was stricken by cholera. He died five days later.

—Hal Marcovitz

Millard Fillmore
Chapter Thirteen

When Millard Fillmore was fifteen years old, his parents sent him to the nearby village of Sparta, New York, to learn the trade of wool-carding. Millard had been a good student in school—whenever he managed to attend—but the Fillmores were nearly destitute; their tiny farm hardly produced crops, and they desperately needed the few dollars their boy's salary as an apprentice would provide to supplement the family's meager income. Young as he was, he was sent to learn a trade because his sister Olive, though older, could not go into an apprenticeship and his brother was even younger than Millard.

Benjamin Hungerford was the man to whom Millard was apprenticed; Hungerford was a family friend who owned a wool-carding factory. Carding is the removing of dirt, twigs, and other impurities from raw wool, then preparing it to be spun. For years, carding was performed by hand, usually by girls and their mothers who would spend long hours combing the raw wool with stiff metal brushes until the fibers were smooth and could be spun into yarn. In 1797, a Massachusetts entrepreneur named Amos Whittemore invented a machine that could card wool, using large wooden implements with metal teeth fixed to cylinders. Each machine could card as much wool as dozens of workers.

Yet it was with some reluctance that Millard Fillmore agreed to work for Hungerford. It was 1815, and war with Great Britain (the War of 1812) had just ended. Millard had been too young to join the army, but as he grew older he harbored dreams of becoming a soldier. However, Millard's father Nathaniel convinced him to take up the trade, and so young Millard made his way to Sparta to become an apprentice to Hungerford.

William Scott, foreman of Hungerford's factory, would soon become Millard's close friend. Scott would later recall his first glimpse of the boy as he entered the factory: "He was dressed in a suit of homespun sheep's gray coat and trousers, wool hat, and stout cowhide boots. His light hair was long, his face was round and chubby, and his demeanor was that of a bright, intelligent, good natured lad, quite sedate, rather slow in his motions, with an air of thoughtfulness that gained my respect."

Millard Fillmore, who was born in 1800, wrote in his autobiography how his parents, a young New York State pioneer family, suffered the privations and hardships common to the frontier. Fillmore worked on his father's farm, became a clothier's apprentice in a carding mill, and attended school infrequently. However, he became fascinated with geography after seeing his first map in a copy of Jedidiah Morse's *The American Universal Geography*. Until the Civil War, most Americans' awareness of geography—and maps—came from Morse's volumes. They had no significant competitors.

Jedidiah Morse (1761–1826) is known as the "father of American geography." Dissatisfied with the treatment of America in the existing English texts, he prepared a series of "geographical lectures" which were issued in 1784 as *Geography Made Easy*, the first geography book published in the United States. By 1820, this famous text had passed through twenty-five editions. So successful was this first effort that Morse began a larger work which he published in 1789 as *The American Geographer* and in its later editions as *The American Universal Geography*. This work passed through at least seven U.S. editions, and almost as many European editions, and firmly established Morse's reputation. Morse also wrote the article "America" for the first American edition of the *Encyclopedia Britannica* (1790). In 1795, Morse published *Elements of Geography* for children. This slim book went through scores of editions. His son Samuel Morse is known as the "father of the telegraph" and the inventor of Morse code.

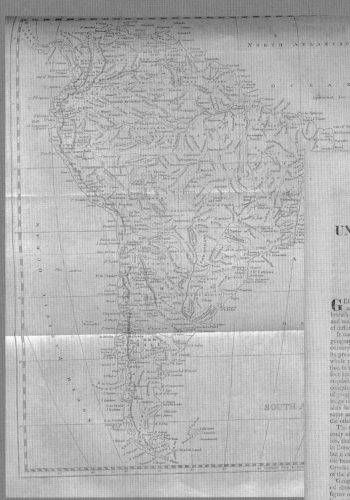

Fillmore wrote in his autobiography that he had learned to read because he "had taken all the schooling the surrounding country could offer." He could read, to be sure, but almost nothing except the Bible and a few spelling books that were available. Years later, he described the family library as "a Bible, a hymn book, and an almanac."

In Colonial days, the almanac was a publication of prime importance for its long-range weather forecasts based on esoteric interpretations of natural phenomena. Beginning as a source for astronomical information, the almanac rapidly grew into an indispensable publication for farmers that contained all sorts of information from recipes to prophecies. The most famous was Benjamin Franklin's *Poor Richard's Almanac*, which first appeared in 1732. It immediately became the most popular book published, second to the Bible. It was unequalled in reputation for proverbs, wit, and wisdom. All almanacs were important publications for they contained information necessary to every American farmer. Seven already were being published in Philadelphia in

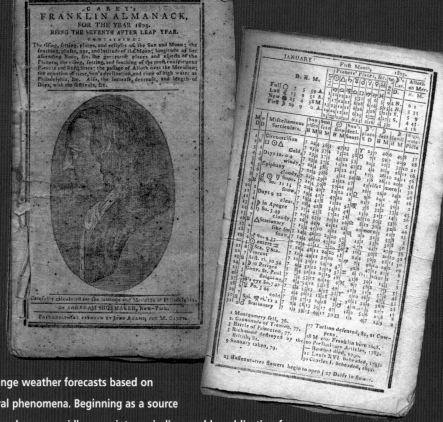

1732, so it seemed unlikely that another would be successful. However, Franklin had new ideas that he felt would insure the success of his venture. Along with the usual information on the weather, tides, eclipses, and medicinal remedies, Franklin printed the maxims and pithy sayings that were even then making him famous. Each edition of Franklin's almanac saw an increase in sales until more than 10,000 were printed annually, approximately one for every hundred people in the colonies.

Franklin stopped writing for the almanac after 1748, when he began to devote most of his time to public affairs. However, his almanac continued to be issued by Matthew Carey, a well-known Philadelphia publisher and writer.

Millard's apprenticeship would last only a few months. Instead of learning the carding trade, his main duties required him to trudge into the woods every day to chop wood to burn in the factory fireplaces. Annoyed with the drudgery of this task, Millard finally confronted Hungerford, telling the factory boss that he hadn't left home to learn how to chop wood. Hungerford ordered Millard to obey him and return to the woodpile. "I will chastise you for your disobedience," Hungerford threatened. In those days, chastisement—or punishment—could include a beating.

Millard refused to step back. Instead, he raised his ax, and said, "You will not chastise me. If you approach me I will split you down."

Hungerford stood before Millard, his body frozen for a moment, then stepped back and walked away. Hungerford soon released Millard from his apprenticeship, permitting him to return home. Years later, Millard, who became the thirteenth president of the United States, had this to say about the incident: "I am inclined to think it was unjustifiable rebellion, or at least my threat of knocking him down was going too far, for I fear I should have executed it; and my only justification or apology is that I have an inborn hatred of injustice and tyranny which I cannot repress."

Born in the most humble of circumstances, Millard entered life on January 7, 1800—the first president of the United States born in the nineteenth century. His parents, Nathaniel and Phoebe Fillmore, had left Vermont in 1798 to settle in central New York State in what was then Onondaga County (now Cayuga County). They raised their children in a crude log cabin in virtual wilderness four miles from their nearest neighbor. Later, Millard would describe his childhood home as "completely shut out from all enterprises of civilization and advancement."

While raising his young family, Nathaniel Fillmore found it very hard to coax crops out of the rocky soil of his farm. In 1802, he lost the farm because of a defect in his deed. The Fillmores were forced to leave the homestead, moving some ten miles to land Millard's father leased near the village of Sempronius, now known as Niles. "My father took a perpetual lease of a small farm of about 130 acres," Fillmore wrote in his autobiography. "[The land] was wholly uncultivated and covered with heavy timber. He built a small log house and commenced clearing the land; and it was at this place and in these pursuits that I first knew anything of life." The Fillmores persevered and soon the land produced crops.

Millard first attended school in a one-room schoolhouse in the nearby village of New Hope. He was either nine or ten when he first took lessons; before this time he probably did not know how to read or write. Moreover, he was hampered by his father's unwillingness to let him attend school for more than a few months in the late fall and winter. In the spring and summer, Nathaniel needed him for labor on the farm.

His first teacher was a Connecticut Yankee named Amos Castle, who found Millard to be a quick learner. Although he was already behind many of his classmates, he advanced quickly and soon impressed Castle with his intelligence and hunger for knowledge. He learned to read with the help of *The American Spelling Book*, written by Noah Webster in 1783. The familiar book with the blue binding was the first attempt to show young students how to read and spell by breaking words into syllables. Some sixty million copies of Webster's spelling book were printed in the more than one hundred years that the book remained in publication.

Clearly, Millard Fillmore was proof that Noah Webster knew how to teach students to spell. After just a few weeks in Castle's school, the teacher awarded Millard a certificate congratulating the young farm boy for "spelling 224 words without missing."

The first novel that Millard read was William Rufus Chetwood's *Voyages and Adventures of Captain Robert Boyle*, the story of a swashbuckling hero who battled pirates, slave traders, and assorted other villains. This book, which was first published in England in 1730, was reprinted almost endlessly for the next century.

But spring soon arrived and Millard's father called the youth back to the fields. At nights, though, Millard was able to teach himself some simple arithmetic and somehow came into the ownership of Jedidiah Morse's *The American Universal Geography*, a school textbook for geography studies that had been in print for about fifteen years by the time Millard obtained his copy. Reading on his own in the Fillmore family cabin, Millard was able to acquaint himself somewhat with the nations of the world and their places on the face of the Earth.

The following winter, Millard enrolled in a Sempronius school led by a Mr. Western, from whom he learned grammar and mathematics. Again, he spent just a few months in school, then was recalled to his father's fields. It would be a pattern repeated each year until Millard was fifteen years old, when he spent those few unpleasant months chopping wood for Benjamin Hungerford.

After returning home from his apprenticeship in Sparta, he again tried to learn the wool-carding trade—this time in a New Hope factory owned by Zaccheus Cheney and Alvan Kellogg, who agreed to take him on for an apprenticeship of five years. This time, Millard found his apprenticeship much more agreeable; Cheney and Kellogg truly did teach him carding and gave him a measure of responsibility. Within a short time, he was maintaining the financial ledgers for the factory.

He was paid $55 a year by Cheney and Kellogg. His agreement with their company gave him time off to help his father on the farm and also attend school in the winter, usually a slow period in the carding business. His hunger for reading remained unquenchable, and finally he had the means to obtain books. In 1817 or 1818, Millard paid $2 to join the Sempronius library, which entitled him access to a small selection of books kept in the librarian's home.

He also bought his own dictionary and propped it up amid the noisy carding machines in the factory, stealing glances at the words and their definitions as he dashed back and forth across the factory floor, feeding the machines and removing the rolls of carded fibers.

In the winter of 1818, when business had slowed in the carding factory, Fillmore found a job as a schoolteacher in the town of Scott, near Cortland, New York. The job paid $10 a month. According to Fillmore, Scott was a "rough and uncultured" place, and the boys at the school were known to make trouble for the teacher. Indeed,

Fillmore obtained the job because the schoolboys had been abusive to the previous teacher and drove him out of town. It didn't take long for the boys of Scott to challenge Millard Fillmore. He very soon found himself in a confrontation with a boy who tested his authority. Fillmore responded by threatening the boy with the fireplace poker. That settled the argument. Fillmore, however, soon learned that parents were distressed that the new teacher had threatened the boy with a poker. At the meeting that followed, Fillmore explained that his action in raising the poker had been self-defense. His explanation was accepted, and he returned to his duties. That spring, after the school year ended, he found work in a sawmill, then returned to the carding factory.

During the following winter, work again fell off in the carding factory. This time, Millard decided to return to school. Although now nineteen and long past the age when most boys left school for work on the family farms or as trade craftsmen, Millard was determined to improve himself intellectually. He enrolled in a school in Sempronius and found room and board with a farm family, for whom he worked as a wood chopper.

It was at the school in Sempronius that he came under the guidance of Abigail Powers, a teacher just two years older than Millard. For Abigail, Millard Fillmore was a student very much out of the ordinary. Certainly, she had taught her share of farm boys in the two years she had been employed as a teacher, but Millard seemed much more intelligent and willing to learn than the other boys in her classes. And, of course, he was much older. She quickly realized that while Millard seemed bright and eager to learn, he lacked refinement. He was polite, but he was at a loss as to how to act in social situations. Abigail became his private tutor, determined to refine his social graces. Soon, she became his fiancée as well.

In 1819, Nathaniel and Phoebe Fillmore moved to a new farm in Montville, about eight miles from Sempronius, where they became tenant farmers on property owned by Judge Walter Wood, who presided over the courts of Cayuga County. Due to the rural nature of the region, Judge Wood had few official duties. Mostly, he was called upon to settle disputes over ownership of properties. In those days, accurate deeds and other property records were a rarity—a fact the Fillmores knew well. After all, a defective deed had caused the Fillmores to lose their first farm.

Nathaniel Fillmore had always been impressed with his son's interest in books and learning. Without telling Millard, Nathaniel asked Judge Wood if he would accept his son as an apprentice lawyer. Wood agreed, and on the young man's first day of work in his office, the judge handed him a copy of William Blackstone's *Commentaries on the Laws of England*.

The British legal scholar Sir William Blackstone had written this series of commentaries on law in 1765, and although the author concentrated on the laws of England, students of law in the United States found much to learn from the text. Blackstone's advocacy for the rule of common law over the power of the king had inspired the framers of the U.S. Constitution. Blackstone wrote of the rights of citizens to "petition the king and parliament to redress grievances." Twenty-five years later, the First Amendment to the Constitution ensured that citizens of the United

COMMENTARIES

ON THE

LAWS

OF

ENGLAND.

BOOK THE FIRST.

BY

WILLIAM BLACKSTONE, Esq.

VINERIAN PROFESSOR OF LAW

AND

SOLICITOR GENERAL TO HER MA

OXFORD,
PRINTED AT THE CLAREND
M. DCC. LXV.

CONTENTS.

INTRODUCTION.

INTRODUCTION.

SECTION THE FIRST.

ON THE STUDY OF THE LAW. *

MR VICE-CHANCELLOR, AND GENTLEMEN OF THE UNIVERSITY,

THE general expectation of so numerous and respectable an audience, the novelty, and (I may add) the importance of the duty required from this chair, must unavoidably be productive of great diffidence and apprehensions in him who has the honour to be placed in it. He must be sensible how much will depend upon his conduct in the infancy of a study, which is now first adopted by public academical authority; which has generally been reputed (however unjustly) of a dry and unfruitful nature; and of which the theoretical, elementary parts have hitherto received a very moderate share of cultivation. He cannot but reflect that, if either his plan of instruction be crude and injudicious, or the execution of it lame and superficial, it will cast a damp upon the farther progress of this most useful and most rational branch of learning; and may defeat for a time the public-spirited

* Read in Oxford at the opening of the Vinerian lectures; 25 Oct. 1758.

A 2

Fillmore wrote how his tenant farming parents uprooted their family almost annually in searching for better land in central New York State. When he was nineteen, Fillmore's father prevailed upon their then landlord, an aged county judge, to "try out Millard for two months as a clerk in his law office." As Fillmore recalled, early the next morning he called at Judge Wood's office. The wrinkled, old man greeted him, "shoved" the first volume of Blackstone's *Commentaries* into his hand, and directed, "Thee will please turn thy attention to this."

Sir William Blackstone's four-volume *Commentaries on the Laws of England* (1765–69) was the first great effort to reduce English common law to a unified and rational system. The preservation of liberty, Blackstone wrote, required a widespread understanding of what the English legal system was all about. Blackstone's *Commentaries* was the dominant law book and the basis of university legal education in both England and America until the 1860s. It is the most important legal treatise ever written in the English language.

Above are the title and preface pages from a facsimile of the first edition of book one, "Of the Rights of Persons." After two months of reading Blackstone, Fillmore admitted that he did not understand the book.

States have the right "to petition the government for a redress of grievances."

To work as an apprentice to Judge Wood, Millard had to gain the permission of Cheney and Kellogg, to whom he still owed another year under his apprenticeship in the carding factory. By now, Millard was a valuable employee of the two partners, and they were opposed to releasing him. They finally agreed to terminate his apprenticeship for the sum of $30, which Millard promised to pay out of his future earnings.

Cheney thought him foolish. "Do you see that young man yonder?" Cheney asked a friend after catching sight of Millard on a New Hope street. "He is, for a sensible young man, pursuing a very foolish course. He has been engaged with me in business for some time. He was far the best apprentice I ever had, and the best workman I ever had. He understands the business perfectly, yet he has abandoned his trade and gone to reading law!"

Millard boarded in Judge Wood's comfortable home, which was to be his compensation for assisting the judge in his practice. Otherwise, he earned a salary as a schoolteacher in Montville, which he used to repay Cheney and Kellogg, and made many trips back to Sempronius to see Abigail. During his apprenticeship with the judge, he read law books before school started in the morning and in the afternoon when classes were finished. His chief duty as Wood's apprentice may have been as a land surveyor—an important duty for a judge whose jurisdiction consisted primarily of settling property disputes.

Millard learned much about the law in his two busy years as an apprentice under Judge Wood, yet he soon found himself bored by the mundane duties Wood assigned him. During his apprenticeship he was employed by Elias Rogers of the town of Moravia to represent him in a lawsuit filed with a justice of the peace, a court official who presides over minor cases. Millard handled the settlement of the case for Rogers, who paid him a fee of $3. When Judge Wood learned of Millard's representation of Rogers, he angrily reprimanded his apprentice because he had not consulted with him before taking the case. Millard protested that he had only performed the work to earn a few dollars, but promised not to accept clients again without Wood's approval. Later, he said, "I don't think Judge Wood knew, or could realize, how important three dollars were to me in those days."

The friction over the Rogers' case prompted Millard to leave Wood's employment. Once again, he would have to pay off his employer because he was leaving before his apprenticeship was completed. He negotiated a settlement with the judge for $65, which he promised to pay out of his future earnings as an attorney. Although his parting with Judge Wood was hardly amicable, Millard would long remember an important piece of advice the judge had given him: "If thee has an ambition for distinction, and can sacrifice everything else to success, the law is the road that leads to honors."

For Millard, the road led to Buffalo, a city on Lake Erie west of Montville, where he found employment as a law clerk in the office of Asa Rice and Joseph Clary. He had little trouble gaining employment, for Buffalo was a growing city. Its several law firms all had heavy case loads and were in dire need of intelligent clerks

PUBLICATIONS
OF THE
BUFFALO
HISTORICAL SOCIETY
VOLUME X

MILLARD FILLMORE PAPERS
VOLUME ONE

EDITED BY
FRANK H. SEVERANCE
SECRETARY OF THE SOCIETY

BUFFALO, NEW YORK:
PUBLISHED BY THE
BUFFALO HISTORICAL SOCIETY
1907

MILLARD FILLMORE'S YOUTH

NARRATIVE OF HIS EARLY YEARS

WRITTEN BY HIMSELF[1]

I have been requested to state some of the early incidents of my life for the benefit of the Buffalo Historical Society; and in compliance with that request I proceed at once to the task. Believing that an humble origin affords no just cause of concealment or shame,—and certainly not, even when fortune has smiled, for vain-boasting and self-glorification, —I shall content myself by stating that I am the second child and eldest son of Nathaniel Fillmore and Phœbe Millard. I was born in Locke (now Summer Hill), Cayuga County, New York, on the seventh day of January, 1800. My father was a native of Bennington, Vermont; and my mother was a native of Pittsfield, Massachusetts. They were early settlers in what was then known as "The Military Tract." At the time of my birth, my father and his brother Calvin, and their wives, occupied the same log house in the midst of the forest, having no neighbor nearer than four miles. About two years after my birth, my father met with what seemed at the time a great misfortune; but was (at least so far as I was concerned) a blessing in disguise. He

[1] This autobiography of the late Millard Fillmore was written in 1871, at the request of the Buffalo Historical Society, and deposited by him in its archives, under seal, not to be opened until after his death. It is printed in Vol. II of the Society's Publications, issued in 1880, but for some years out of print.

MILLARD FILLMORE'S YOUTH. 5

When I was about ten years old, a man was employed by the name of Amos Castle, who gave us some instruction in writing and arithmetic, and drilled us most thoroughly in Webster's spelling-book. I think I went through that book without missing in the spelling of a word; but I did not learn the definition of a single one. In fact, there was no such thing as a dictionary in school, and I had never seen one. From about the age of ten or eleven, I could not be spared from the farm during the summer, and therefore, only attended school for two or three months in the winter. Consequently, I forgot nearly as much during the summer as I learned in the winter. I, however, acquired some knowledge of arithmetic, and read Dwight's old geography of questions and answers enough to have acquired some knowledge of geography, had there been any such thing as a map or atlas in school; but I never saw either till I was nineteen years of age.

When I was about twelve or thirteen, some effort was made to organize a school under our present admirable system of common schools; and after that there was some improvement in our teachers. One scholar had a copy of Morse's geography, which he permitted me to look at, and I devoured it with the greatest avidity. I recollect well the impression made upon me by the account given of Bruce's travels in Abyssinia.

I continued thus to work upon the farm in summer, till I was in my fifteenth year. During that time, being large of my age and unusually strong, I learned to plow, to hoe, to chop, to log and clear land, to mow, to reap, and, finally, to do all kinds of work which is usually done in clearing and cultivating a new farm. But my father's misfortune in losing his land, and the scarcely less misfortune of having a hard, clayey soil for cultivation, gave him a great distaste for farming; and he was, therefore, anxious that his sons should follow some other occupation. His means did not justify him or them in aspiring to any profession, and, therefore, he wished them to learn trades. In the fall of 1814, a neighbor had been drafted into the military service for

Fillmore left the White House in 1853. In those days, there were no national presidential libraries that collected the public and private papers of the nation's chief executives. In subsequent years, Fillmore was the first chancellor of the University of Buffalo, a founder of the Buffalo Historical Society and its first president, a founder of the Buffalo General Hospital, and a volunteer in various other civic, educational, and philanthropic endeavors.

Approximately twenty years after his death in 1874, Frank H. Severance, the secretary of the Buffalo Historical Society, collected Fillmore's scattered private papers as well as reminiscences of those who knew the former president. (The Society had asked Fillmore to write his autobiography in 1871. He stopped after about fifteen pages that deal with his youth and education. These pages are the primary source for this period of the former president's life.) In 1907, under Severance's direction, the Buffalo Historical Society published the *Millard Fillmore Papers*, including the brief autobiography, in two volumes.

who could help the attorneys prepare precise summaries. He earned no salary under Rice and Clary, and again had to take a job as a teacher. Nevertheless, Rice and Clary helped prepare Millard for his bar examination, and in February 1823 all his years of hard work and self-denial finally paid off when he passed the examination and was permitted to practice law in the state of New York.

The years of poverty would soon be behind Millard Fillmore. He became a busy lawyer, opening his own practice in the town of Aurora, where his parents had bought a farm. In 1826 he married Abigail; his seven years' labor had gained him his bride. Moving back to Buffalo in 1830, he launched his political career. Two years later, he was elected to the state assembly. Though he was elected largely on the basis of the political party to which he belonged, he was responsible for laws that banned the practice of jailing debtors. He also became a protégé of New York Whig newspaper publisher and political powerbroker Thurlow Weed, who guided Fillmore's career into the New York

State Legislature and then the United States Congress. In 1840, the Whigs captured control of the U.S. House of Representatives, and Fillmore become chairman of the powerful Ways and Means Committee. In that capacity, he took the lead in framing the protectionist Tariff Act of 1842.

Weed pushed him to run for governor of New York. Against Fillmore's better judgment, he ran in 1844 and was defeated by Silas Wright, the good friend of former president Martin Van Buren. (Fillmore attributed his defeat to "the Abolitionists and foreign Catholics.") Three years later Fillmore was elected comptroller of New York, which is the state's highest fiscal office. He had held office for just a year when he was selected to join Zachary Taylor on the Whigs' presidential ticket. The presidential nomination of Taylor, a hero of the Mexican War, had angered Northern Whigs because Taylor was a Southerner and slaveholder. Fillmore was selected as the candidate for vice president in part because he was a Northerner who gave geographical balance to the ticket. He owed his nomination for vice president to the influence of Henry Clay, who, angered at the choice of Taylor, refused to accept Abbot Lawrence, the Massachusetts cotton manufacturer, as the nominee for vice president. Clay declared he would not "have cotton at both ends of the ticket." Fillmore and Taylor never met until after the election, and when they did meet, they concluded that they didn't like each other.

Taylor's presidency was brief. He died in 1850, before the most important piece of legislation produced by Congress during his tenure reached the White House: the Fugitive Slave Act. The act, which would give Southern slaveholders more power to seek the return of slaves who had escaped to the Northern states, was drafted by Senator Henry Clay as part of what became known as the "Compromise of 1850." In exchange, Southern legislators had agreed to admit California into the Union as a free state, where slavery was prohibited. Although Taylor was a slaveholder, he wanted to preserve the United States, and made it clear before his death that he would not sign the bill. However, by the time the legislation reached the president's desk, Fillmore was the occupant of the White House. Although Fillmore and his Cabinet also wanted to preserve the Union, he signed the bill, believing it would help avoid Civil War.

The Abolitionist wing of the Whig Party seethed when Fillmore signed the Fugitive Slave Act. They refused to support him in the 1852 election, denying him the Whig nomination. It would be the last election for the Whig Party, which disintegrated after its defeat that year. Many former Whigs now joined a new party for the 1856 election—the Republican Party. Fillmore, though, joined the American Party, a coalition of former Whigs and anti-immigration zealots. They were nicknamed the "Know-Nothing Party" because party members, when asked questions by outsiders, were told to respond only "I know nothing." The party lasted only briefly. In the presidential election of 1856, Fillmore finished a distant third. He soon retired from politics.

Fillmore remained active in his retirement, eventually becoming the first chancellor of the University of Buffalo—a rewarding achievement for a man whose own education had suffered because of the terrible poverty of his youth.

—Hal Marcovitz

Franklin Pierce
Chapter Fourteen

He was a curly, blue-eyed child with "a sweet expression of face," according to his friend Nathaniel Hawthorne. In the opinion of many historians, young Franklin Pierce grew to become America's handsomest president. Photographs depict a dour but striking face with thin lips and a fine, straight nose beneath shocks of dark, wavy hair and protruding brows. He appears to be an intelligent, sensitive man of social graces, but with a countenance singed by personal grief. Pierce was a president buffeted by unhappiness and ill-prepared for the gathering storm of division that soon would overcome his nation. Standing a frail five feet, ten inches, harried by lung disease, Franklin Pierce was not destined for long life. Perhaps it was a mercy. From 1853, the year he took office as then America's youngest president, until his death sixteen years later, he would suffer a downward spiral of unpopularity, failure, bitterness, and sorrow.

One weekend in 1816, twelve-year-old Franklin faced a crisis that seemed far more unbearable to him than all the problems that ever could beset a head of state: he was homesick. His parents, determined that he would have a better education than they, had enrolled him at an academy in Hancock, New Hampshire, about fifteen miles from his hometown of Hillsborough. It was his first experience of leaving home, and he soon decided Hancock was not for him. Early that Sunday morning, he walked home. His family arrived from church to find him waiting with a carefully prepared argument of why he needed no further schooling.

To Franklin's puzzlement, his father listened quietly. Benjamin Pierce did not punish his son, or even scold him. After dinner, the parent hitched the horse and carriage and took Franklin for a drive. Instantly, the boy's dismay returned—they were on the road to Hancock. Halfway there, the father deposited Franklin at roadside, turned the horse, and silently drove away. Forlorn, Franklin had little choice but return to prep school and adjust.

Lessons of life were often harsh and usually effective in early America. They had to be. In New Hampshire's aptly named "Land of Hills," this kind of upbringing forged the likes of Daniel Webster and John Stark. Webster, twenty-four years old at Franklin's

Bridgton

CATALOGUE

OF THE

OFFICERS AND STUDENTS

OF

BOWDOIN COLLEGE,

MAINE,

OCTOBER, 1822.

—

BRUNSWICK:
JOSEPH GRIFFIN.
1822.

BOWDOIN COLLEGE.

MARCH, 1822.

—ooo—

TERMS OF ADMISSION.

Candidates for admisssion into the Freshman Class are required to write Latin grammatically, and to be well versed in Geography, in Walsh's Arithmetic' Cicero's Select Orations, the Bucolics, Georgics, and Aeneid of Virgil, Sallust, the Greek Testament, and Collectanea Græca Minora. They must produce certificates of their good moral character. The usual time for examination is the day after Commencement.—Candidates for admission into the other classes will be examined also in the books, which have been studied by the class, into which admission is requested.—Scholars from other Colleges, before they can be examined, must produce a certificate of their regular dismission.

COURSE OF STUDY.

FRESHMAN CLASS.

First Term. Xenophon in Græca Majora; Livy; Arithmetic in Webber.
Second Term. Græca Majora, (Vol. i.); Livy; Arithmetic continued.
Third Term. Græca Majora continued; Livy finished (5 books); Murray's English Grammar; Blair's Rhetoric; Review of the studies of the year.
During the whole year. Weekly translations into Latin and Greek; private Declamations; Recitations from the Bible every Sunday evening.

Franklin Pierce enrolled in Bowdoin College in October 1820. He was sixteen years old. In order to matriculate, Pierce had to write grammatically correct Latin and to sight translate Cicero's *Orations* and Virgil's *Aeneid*. The freshman year was divided into three parts. Reading assignments were in the Greek and Latin classics, plus each student had to master advanced arithmetic and English grammar. Mandatory Bible reading occurred every Sunday evening.

Located along the Maine coast in Brunswick, Bowdoin was chartered in 1794. The college admitted its first students in 1802 and awarded its first degrees in 1806.

The page on the left is the handwritten record of the Bowdoin College Library that list "Pierce" and the books that he withdrew, October 1821 through April 20, 1823. Among the books Pierce borrowed from the library was Lewis and Clark's *Expedition* (two vols.) [*History of the Expedition Under the Command of Captains Lewis and Clark to the Sources of the Missouri, Thence Across the Rocky Mountains and Down the River Columbia to the Pacific Ocean Performed During the Years* 1804–06]. This was the first edition (1814) of the most famous of all western travel narratives.

Pierce also withdrew from the library Oliver Goldsmith's popularly written book *Roman History, From the Foundations of the City of Rome to the Destruction of the Western Empire* (1769) and Simon Ockley's *History of the Saracens* (1718). The latter is an adventure book that describes the Saracens, a medieval Islamic people, their battles, sieges, religion, and customs. He borrowed books in Latin such as the illustrated *Antiquitatum Romanarum Corpus Absolutissimum cum Notis Doctissimis ac Locupletissimus Thomae Dempstieri, J.C.* [*A Complete Book of Roman Artifacts with an authoritative introduction by Thomas Dempstieri*] (1743).

Theodore L. Moody was Pierce's roommate at Bowdoin for two years. His library record from July 29, 1823 through June 30, 1824 (right) informs us that he borrowed and renewed, and borrowed several additional times, the Scottish philosopher David Hume's two-volume *Essays and Treatises on Several Subjects* (1767). Moody also renewed various volumes by British political theorist Edmund Burke at least ten times. These handwritten library records have survived more than one hundred eighty years. It is interesting to wonder if today's college library records will endure as long.

There were thirteen students in Pierce's class of 1824. In addition to a $24 yearly tuition, there was an added library fee of about $1.50. Room and board cost approximately $2 per week. A mandatory student debate on an assigned topic was held each Wednesday afternoon. All students, in alphabetical rotation, had to argue a given topic.

birth, was preparing for a law career that would lead him to fame as one of the country's greatest orators of all time. Crusty Brigadier General Stark, one of the most celebrated militia commanders of the Revolutionary War, by that time was retired to his farm.

Benjamin Pierce, Franklin's father, is far lesser known today but was highly respected throughout New England. He was a self-made man who rose to prominence from an upbringing as a poor colonial farmer. He had little education but steadfast conviction and courage. Raised by an uncle, seventeen-year-old Benjamin is said to have been plowing a field when he received the electrifying news of skirmishes between colonists and British soldiers at Lexington and Concord, Massachusetts—the outbreak of the American Revolution. It was April 1775. He literally walked from the field, took up arms, and spent the next seven years fighting for freedom. After the end of the Revolution, his meager soldier's pay allowed him to buy fifty acres near Hillsborough. Benjamin set about clearing his land, building a log home beside a creek, and finding himself a wife. His first, Elizabeth Andrews, died less than a year after their marriage. Two years later, he married Anna Kendrick. As their family grew, so did the local prestige of honest, plainspoken Ben Pierce. He was made an officer in the Hillsborough militia and was elected to the New Hampshire legislature. Later, he served as county sheriff and postmaster.

Soon after Franklin's birth, on November 23, 1804, the family built a larger home in Lower Hillsborough Village. The new republic offered hope for prosperity, and the Pierces understood what would be required for their nine children to achieve it: education. Meanwhile, the parents instilled characteristics that were hallmarks of early nineteenth-century New Englanders. His mother saw to it that Franklin grew firmly in the Episcopalian faith. His father passed along—as much by example as by words—love of country and the importance of upholding the law of the land. According to biographer Nathaniel Hawthorne, the youthful Franklin was remembered in old Hillsborough as kind, upright, and "very delightful." At the same time, he was a typical, fun-loving boy who roamed the forests and skated on the ponds in winter. He became an eager fisher—a passion he kept throughout his life.

When Franklin was seven, mounting tension between the United States and Great Britain led the two countries into another war. One of Franklin's older brothers and a brother-in-law served in the army during the War of 1812. At home in New Hampshire, the war was Franklin's introduction to politics. He observed his father's public and private discussions on the course of the conflict and other affairs of the nation. Benjamin Pierce, staunchly anti-Federalist, supported President Thomas Jefferson and the fledgling Democratic-Republican Party. Franklin did not understand what the conflict was all about, but he began to see that confusing complications could arise in a democracy when differing regional and economic interests clashed.

Franklin attended the regular Hillsborough school until he was twelve. Then he was sent to college prep schools, first in Hancock and then in Francestown, New Hampshire. He got along well with other students and went out of his way to earn their friendship. In one case, he reportedly spent his daily recess periods for weeks on end helping a lagging schoolmate catch up with class work. Hawthorne later wrote of Franklin's "sweetness of disposition and cordial sympathy," but he also had the reputation of a prankster who loved to romp and tussle with his cronies, sometimes at the expense of the furniture.

At Francestown Academy, Franklin labored under the stern instruction of Simeon Ingersoll Bard, "a walking dictionary and a strong disciplinarian," in the words of biographer Roy Franklin Nichols. Bard quizzed his young charges relentlessly until they knew their Latin, Greek, chemistry, geography, and arithmetic.

Their father had sent Franklin's older brother Ben to Dartmouth College, but then decided the politics of the Dartmouth administration and faculty weren't to his liking. Specifically, Dartmouth at the time was largely under the sway of Federalists (including Daniel Webster). Franklin, the father decided, would attend Bowdoin College in Brunswick, a small lumber town near the Maine coast. Bowdoin was a new college, in operation less than twenty years when Franklin arrived, but it would attain prestige in coming generations. At the time Franklin attended, Bowdoin consisted of two campus buildings and a plain chapel that doubled as the college library.

In autumn 1820, Franklin's parents personally accompanied him to Brunswick in the family's two-wheeled, horse-drawn carriage and settled him into a boarding house. He was the only freshman among the six student residents there, but he was not intimidated. He looked ahead eagerly to his years at Bowdoin. "My spirits were exuberant," he recalled later. "I was far from my home without restraint except such as the government of a college imposed."

Nineteen students were in his freshman class; five would drop out by their senior year. The likable sixteen-year-old quickly made many friends. By far the most important in his life was Nathaniel Hawthorne, who enrolled a year after Franklin. Hawthorne would become one of America's most famous authors, writing such books as *The Scarlet Letter*, *The House of the Seven Gables*, *Tanglewood Tales*, and *Twice-Told Tales*. Today, the writings of Nathaniel Hawthorne are much better known to Americans than is the presidential record of Franklin Pierce. Other classmates at Bowdoin during the early 1820s included Henry Wadsworth Longfellow, who would become one of America's best-loved poets, and John P. Hale, who eventually would pose fierce political opposition for the future president.

Much later, Hawthorne wrote a biography to help Pierce's presidential election campaign. The author recalled of his old friend, "He was then a youth, with the boy and man in him, vivacious, mirthful, slender, of a fair complexion, with light hair that had a curl in it: his bright and cheerful aspect made a kind of sunshine, both as regarded its radiance and its warmth; insomuch that no shyness of disposition, in his associates, could well resist its influence."

The Bowdoin student body was divided into two societies or, as Hawthorne defined them, "institutions": the "respectable conservative" and the "progressive." Both he and Pierce were progressives. Pierce became a skilled debater and took a keen interest in politics. He was also impressed by the writings of British

Pierce had to write grammatically correct Latin and to sight translate Cicero's *Orations* and Virgil's *Aeneid*.

In May 1823, Bowdoin College held its annual spring "exhibition," or Classical oratorical program. Pierce was chosen to participate. He wrote and read this essay in Latin—*De triumphis Romanorum* (The Roman Triumphs). According to his letters, he was "greatly relieved when it was over."

The fact that both Henry Wadsworth Longfellow and Nathaniel Hawthorne were students at Bowdoin during most of Pierce's collegiate years has made descriptions of the college plentiful. All biographers of these men give accounts of Bowdoin student life during the 1820s. Pierce exchanged letters with most of his classmates throughout his life, fulfilling a mutual pledge "of constant and continuous correspondence."

In 1852, the Democratic Party nominated Franklin Pierce as its candidate for president. During the campaign, Pierce wrote letters of appreciation to supporters but otherwise followed the advice of Democratic elders to do as little as possible and to say almost nothing about his views on any topic. With Pierce's approval, his college friend Nathaniel Hawthorne wrote the "authorized" campaign biography, *The Life of Franklin Pierce* (144 pages). About 13,000 copies were printed by late September. The New York City Democratic Party (Tammany Hall) purchased 5,000 copies for "immediate distribution." During the presidential campaign, Pierce and Hawthorne attended the fiftieth anniversary of the admission of the first students to Bowdoin. Among the new president's first appointments was that of Hawthorne to be American consul at Liverpool.

LIFE

OF

FRANKLIN PIERCE.

BY

NATHANIEL HAWTHORNE.

BOSTON:
TICKNOR, REED, AND FIELDS.
M DCCC LII.

---

14   LIFE OF

in aiding him in his lessons. These attributes, proper to a generous and affectionate nature, have remained with him through life. Lending their color to his deportment, and softening his manners, they are, perhaps, even now, the characteristics by which most of those who casually meet him would be inclined to identify the man. But there are other qualities, not then developed, but which have subsequently attained a firm and manly growth, and are recognized as his leading traits among those who really know him. Franklin Pierce's development, indeed, has always been the reverse of premature; the boy did not show the germ of all that was in the man, nor, perhaps, did the young man adequately foreshow the mature one.

In 1820, at the age of sixteen, he became a student of Bowdoin College, at Brunswick, Maine. It was in the autumn of the next year, that the author of this memoir entered the class below him; but our college reminiscences, however interesting to the parties concerned, are not exactly the material for a biography. He was then a youth, with the boy and man in him, vivacious, mirthful, slender, of a fair complexion, with light hair that had a curl in it: his bright and cheerful aspect made a kind of sunshine, both as regarded its radiance and its warmth; insomuch that no shyness of disposition, in his associates, could well resist its influence. We soon became acquainted, and were more philosopher John Locke. He joined the Athenaean Society, one of Bowdoin's two literary clubs, and was elected captain of the military drill company, the Bowdoin Cadets. Hawthorne described the boy commander's "air and step of a veteran…as well became the son of a revolutionary hero." In fact, until well into his college years, Pierce seems to have contemplated an army career.

One of Pierce's closest friends was an older student named Zenas Caldwell, "a pure-minded, studious, devoutly religious character…with the authority of a grave and sagacious turn of mind." Caldwell's strong religious beliefs had a marked impact on Pierce; during their senior year, when they roomed together, they prayed each night on their knees before going to bed.

Caldwell apparently typified many Bowdoin students, who tended to be significantly older than the lad from Hillsborough and, unlike Pierce, were working to pay for their own education. Naturally, they were more inclined than he to take their studies very seriously and learn all they could for the money they were paying. For the first two years, Pierce proved far more adroit in social activities than learning. "Carefree and irresponsible," Nichols chronicled, "he trailed along, getting his work from others if he couldn't do it himself." On at least one occasion, he openly admitted to a professor in class that he'd solved a difficult algebra problem by copying a fellow student's work.

As a result, Pierce's grades dropped him to the bottom of his class. "It could have been no easy task," Hawthorne reflected sympathetically, "to hold successful rivalry with students so much in earnest as these were." By other accounts, though, Pierce's descent into the academic cellar was his own doing. When he first read the student list at the beginning of his third year and saw his name at the bottom, he recoiled angrily and vowed to abort his education. But then he buckled down to his books, encouraged by Caldwell and other chums. He steadily improved his record until by graduation he ranked near the top among his peers.

Meanwhile, his ingrained patriotic and Episcopalian values from childhood took root. Hawthorne affirmed that during his final years at Bowdoin, Pierce's "habits of attention, and obedience to college discipline, were of the strictest character."

Franklin Pierce soon began to consider seriously what he might best be suited to do in life. Just as importantly, he began actually contributing to society. At Caldwell's request, Pierce spent the six-week winter break of his junior year teaching at the wilderness schoolhouse in Hebron, Maine. He stayed with the Caldwell family, who treated him as an honored guest. In return, he spent fireside evenings tutoring Caldwell's younger brother, who hoped to attend college. Perhaps the strongest evidence of his newfound dedication was his decision not to go home for the spring break that year. Instead, he remained on campus to prepare for the summer term.

College life two centuries ago was much different from today. Students had to follow rules that would appall their modern-day successors. At Bowdoin, they could not leave the vicinity of Brunswick or nearby Topsham unless their parents requested permission for them, could not shoot pool or play cards, could not "attend any theatrical entertainment or any idle show in Brunswick or Topsham," could not shout or sing loudly (which would dishonor "the character of a literary institution"), and could go hunting and fishing only with permission. Weekends were by no means a time for pleasure. To the contrary, the rules of Bowdoin stipulated: "Students must be in their rooms Saturday and Sunday evenings and abstain from diversions of every kind. They who profane the Sabbath by unnecessary business, visiting or receiving visits, or by walking abroad, or by any amusement, or in other ways, may be admonished or suspended." Students were fined for missing classes and daily prayers. The penalty for not sitting erect and attentive at chapel was fifty cents—a hefty fee in 1820, when a week's room and board cost about two dollars.

Six days of each week brought the same regimen: chapel at eight-thirty, an hour-long class at nine, an hour-long study period at ten, another class at eleven, two hours for lunch and exercise. Except on Saturday, students spent most of the afternoon in private study, with a final late-afternoon class followed by evening prayers conducted by the college president. Courses included arithmetic, English grammar, Latin and Greek translations, history, and "forensics" (speech/debates). In time, algebra, geometry, chemistry, religion, philosophy, and mineralogy were added to Pierce's subjects.

Boarding facilities were plain and chilly in winter. Students read by candlelight. Classrooms were likewise barren. On cold days, students had a practical incentive for arriving at class early rather than late: they coveted the seats closest to the fireplace. The library opened at noon each day for exactly one hour. Books in those years were held in great value, and check-out policies were strictly limited— freshmen, for example, could take out just one book at a time.

The school year was divided into three terms. It began in October and ended in early September, with a six-week vacation in winter, three-week break in spring, and four weeks in autumn between the old year and the new. Tuition, board, and other expenses totaled about two hundred dollars a year.

Despite the Bowdoin regimen, Pierce found time to enjoy the Maine coastal setting. He loved to walk the forest paths with his friends and explore along the Androscoggin River. They went swimming in fair weather, picked berries, and fished the river and hunted squirrels and birds. For amusement, they visited the riverside shanty of an old fortuneteller and brazenly frequented the village tavern in defiance of campus rules.

A pressing concern among college students today is whether they may keep a car on campus. Similarly, Franklin Pierce apparently lobbied his father for permission to keep a horse at Bowdoin—a privilege the elder Pierce granted during Franklin's senior year.

Franklin had risen high enough in his grades that he was chosen to give one of his class's commencement speeches. He was deeply disappointed that his father

Bowdoin College campus, 1823, oil on canvas, by John G. Brown

Bowdoin College is named for the Revolutionary War–era American statesman James Bowdoin (1726–90) who also was the first president of the American Academy of Arts and Sciences (founded in 1780). In 1794, his son James donated land and money to establish the college named in honor of his father. During their first week on campus, Bowdoin students follow a tradition by signing the same Matriculation Book as did Hawthorne, Longfellow, and Pierce.

did not attend his graduation, opting instead to attend a reception in Portsmouth, New Hampshire, for the Marquis de Lafayette, hero of the Revolution.

After graduating from Bowdoin in 1824, Pierce went to work as a clerk for several lawyers and judges in succession. In those times, many aspiring lawyers learned their profession not by attending law school, but by literally "reading law" under the tutelage of an established barrister. They had to familiarize themselves with *Commentaries on the Laws of England*, Sir William Blackstone's classic legal reference, and to master the details of their state and national constitutions.

Pierce also attended law school in Northampton, Massachusetts. Then, after two more clerkships, he was admitted to the bar in 1827. He began his law practice in Hillsborough—and lost his first case. It was a healthy jolt of realism that, in Hawthorne's words, "did but serve to make him aware of the latent resources of his mind."

Only twenty-three years old, Franklin Pierce was embarked on a remarkable career that would lift him from the losing counsel's humble table in a Hillsborough courtroom to the White House in Washington. The same year he became a lawyer, his father was elected governor of New Hampshire. Benjamin Pierce's wide-ranging influence in regional affairs of state would benefit his son's vocation. For his own part, Franklin Pierce had acquired at Bowdoin the public speaking and debating skills he would need for what was to come. He already possessed the outgoing personality that could build popularity among voters. He was a fine dresser, a young man who was fun to be around, who liked to please everyone, and who easily won the trust of new acquaintances.

At twenty-four, Pierce was elected to the New Hampshire state legislature. Four years later, he was elected to the first of two terms in Congress. In 1836, he became the youngest U.S. senator of his time.

Just before completing his Senate term, he resigned and returned to law practice. This he did at the urging of his wife Jane, a fragile, shy woman he had met at Bowdoin and married in 1834. Jane Pierce hated politics, and throughout his career, she discouraged her husband from the statesman's life.

During the 1840s, Pierce developed into one of the most persuasive lawyers in New England. Citizens from near and far packed the courtroom to hear him argue cases. It was a talent that would prove invaluable a decade later in his bid for president. Another priceless credential for national politics was a military record. Although Pierce's experiences in the Mexican War (1846–48) were less than heroic, he took his place among the popular returning veterans.

He was not the favored presidential candidate at the Democratic national convention in Baltimore in June 1852. After the four leading contenders repeatedly failed to win a majority of delegates' votes, he won the nomination as a compromise choice. He went on to defeat the Whig candidate, General Winfield Scott, in the general election.

Only forty-eight years old, Franklin had become the foremost American. But his was a tragic life. He and his wife lost all three of their sons in childhood. The third, Bennie, was killed in a train wreck in January 1853, just two months before Pierce took office as president.

Most historians consider Franklin Pierce one of America's weakest presidents. The great irony is that during his term in office (1853–57) the United States was unusually prosperous. The country was expanding steadily westward, connected by spreading railway systems, and factories were mass-producing a variety of products.

But a fatal divisiveness was brewing between North and South over the slavery issue. In a way, the president seemed in a unique position to bridge the differences between regions. A New Englander, Pierce nevertheless had strong political friendships with southern statesmen. He insisted compromise was the answer—but in the turbulent political arena of the 1850s, compromise only fueled the fire of dissension. Above all, Franklin was a patriot sworn to uphold the Constitution and preserve the federal union. Toward that end, he took great care—too much care, historians judge—to appease the South in the escalating crisis. He made significant proslavery political appointments and decisions. This steadily lost support for both him and the Democratic Party in the northern states. His hopes of a second term were doomed. Four years after he left office, the nation went to war. Franklin Pierce became what some historians call "the forgotten president."

Jane Pierce died in 1863, still in her fifties. A few months later, Pierce accompanied his old school friend Nathaniel Hawthorne to New England's idyllic White Mountains. Hawthorne was in failing health, and they hoped the secluded environment would help him. It did not; Hawthorne died one night in a bedroom next to Franklin Pierce's room. While others had forsaken the former president, the Bowdoin underclassman had remained faithful. Now he was gone.

Franklin Pierce's own death came in 1869 in Concord, New Hampshire.

—Daniel E. Harmon

James Buchanan
Chapter Fifteen

Weary from long nights of carousing, a bored young man named James Buchanan endured his geography teacher's lectures with no small measure of contempt. Buchanan was not alone. Virtually every student who took classes under Dr. Robert Davidson would report their hatred for the man who not only lectured them in the classroom, but served as head of the Dickinson College faculty as well.

Another of Davidson's students, Roger B. Taney, remembered the teacher years later. "He was not harsh or ill-natured in his intercourse with us, but he was formal and solemn and precise and, in short, was always the pedagogue in school and out of school," wrote Taney, who had studied at Dickinson College fourteen years before Buchanan. Taney, like Buchanan, would go on to a career that would culminate in high public office; he became chief justice of the Supreme Court of the United States.

Buchanan, Taney, and other students who passed through Davidson's classes were required to memorize and recite a poem written by Davidson, which purported to explain the mysteries of the globe in a few terse lines. The students thought the exercise was ridiculous; nonetheless, they memorized the verse. The poem included these lines:

> Round the globe now to rove, and its surface survey,
> Oh, youth of America, hasten away;
> Bid adieu for awhile to the toys you desire,
> Earth's beauties to view, and its wonders admire.

"Nothing, I think, impaired the respect of the class for Dr. Davidson more than his acrostic," recalled Taney. "It was so often…repeated among us in derision.""

Buchanan was even less enamored with Davidson's teaching methods than Taney had been. By far the brightest of the students at Dickinson, the sixteen-year-old Buchanan found that it didn't require much in the way of study to pass his courses. Instead, he spent his nights not poring over the day's lessons, but in the taverns of Carlisle, Pennsylvania, drinking ale and smoking cigars in blatant violation of college rules. "Without much natural tendency to become dissipated," he later

In 1807, James Buchanan entered the junior class of Dickinson College in what was then a frontier town—Carlisle, Pennsylvania. Dickinson had been founded in 1784 through the efforts of Benjamin Rush, the revolutionary statesman, who believed that a college "with an open Bible" was needed in Pennsylvania west of the Appalachians. Buchanan found the school in "wretched condition" with no "efficient discipline." His behavior at Dickinson was far from exemplary. "I engaged in every sort of extravagance and mischief," he wrote. He was expelled in 1808 but was readmitted after pledging good behavior to his minister, a college trustee. Buchanan completed his senior year, graduating in September 1809. "I left college," he wrote, "feeling little attachment to the Alma Mater."

Forty-two students were enrolled at Dickinson in 1807—eight in the senior class, nineteen in Buchanan's junior, and the remainder were freshmen or assigned to the Latin preparatory school. (The college did not yet include a sophomore year.) The entire teaching staff included three instructors. Robert Davidson, an ordained Presbyterian minister, was the president. He taught history, geography, and philosophy. Davidson was particularly fond of astronomy, having written a short pamphlet on geography and astronomy in rhyme that each Dickinson student had to purchase and memorize. John Hayes was in charge of languages, and James McCormick handled mathematics. McCormick also lodged and boarded half a dozen students at his home, including Buchanan. "Mr. McCormick and his wife were as kind to us as if they had been our parents," recalled a Buchanan classmate. "[He] sometimes seemed quite distressed when, upon examining a pupil, he found him not quite as learned as he was himself."

Two of Buchanan's handwritten college notebooks have survived, both from 1808—"Lecture Notes on Trigonometry, Surveying, and Navigation," and "Questions and Answers on Mathematics, Astronomy and Natural Philosophy."

Illustrated above is a page in Buchanan's handwriting for an 1808 paper on navigation required in Professor McCormick's class. Next to it is a page from the noted astronomer Nathaniel Bowditch's book *The New American Practical Navigator* (c.1802 edition). This is an example of rote education so common in early eighteenth-century American colleges. Usually, there was a shortage of textbooks. Students were required to copy—and at the same time to memorize—from the few books available to the instructor.

explained, "and chiefly from the example of others, and in order to be considered a clever and spirited youth, I engaged in every sort of extravagance and mischief."

When his first year at Dickinson was completed, Buchanan passed his final examinations with ease and returned to his family's farm in nearby Mercersburg to relax for a few weeks while awaiting the start of the winter term and another year of rowdy behavior.

On one pleasantly warm, late summer day in September, Buchanan suffered a sudden and rude shock. There was a knock on the door. His father James answered and was handed a note by a messenger. The elder Buchanan opened the envelope and read the contents of the note silently to himself. It was clear from the man's expression that the correspondence contained the gravest of news. Without uttering a word, James glared at his son, tossed him the note, and stormed out of the room.

Young James read the letter, in which Dr. Davidson informed James's father that his vain, sarcastic, and carousing son would not be invited back for another year at Dickinson College. In fact, wrote Davidson, the boy would have been given the boot earlier if it had not been for the respect the faculty held for his father. "They had borne with me as best they could until that period," Buchanan recalled, "but they would not receive me again, and…the letter was written to [my father] to save him the mortification of sending me back and having me rejected. Mortified to the soul, I at once determined upon my course."

The story of Abraham Lincoln's humble beginnings are known to every school child—how the nation's sixteenth president was born in a log cabin and learned to read by the light of a cooking fire is part of the story of America. Less well-known, though, is the fact that Lincoln's immediate predecessor in the White House was also born in a log cabin on the edge of what was then America's frontier.

James Buchanan was born April 23, 1791, in Cove Gap, Pennsylvania, about one hundred and forty miles west of Philadelphia. At the time, Cove Gap was one of the last crossroads towns on the trail into America's wilderness. As such, the busiest place in town was the trading post and warehouse run by John Tom. Pioneers, trappers, homesteaders, soldiers, and others heading west all stopped at "Stony Batter," which is what Tom called his store, to take on supplies.

Tom's assistant at Stony Batter was James Buchanan Sr., a hard-working Presbyterian from County Donegal in the northern part of Ireland. Buchanan had emigrated to America in 1783 at the invitation of an uncle, Joshua Russell, who owned a tavern in Gettysburg. Buchanan arrived in the port of Philadelphia in the summer of 1783; he was met by his uncle who promised to look after the young man. They returned to Gettysburg, where Buchanan lived off the charity of Uncle Joshua only briefly. The ambitious, intelligent and industrious young immigrant was anxious to make his own way, and soon learned of an employment opportunity at John Tom's trading post some forty miles west of Gettysburg.

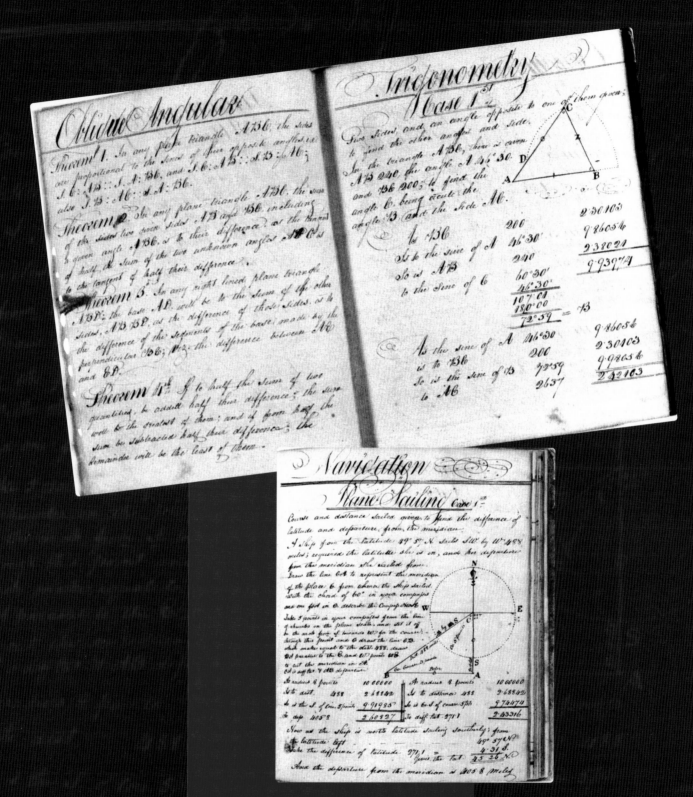

These pages are from James Buchanan's 1808 notebooks on navigation and mathematics. Buchanan found his courses at Dickinson College dull, and his memoirs are most uncomplimentary toward the school and its teaching staff.

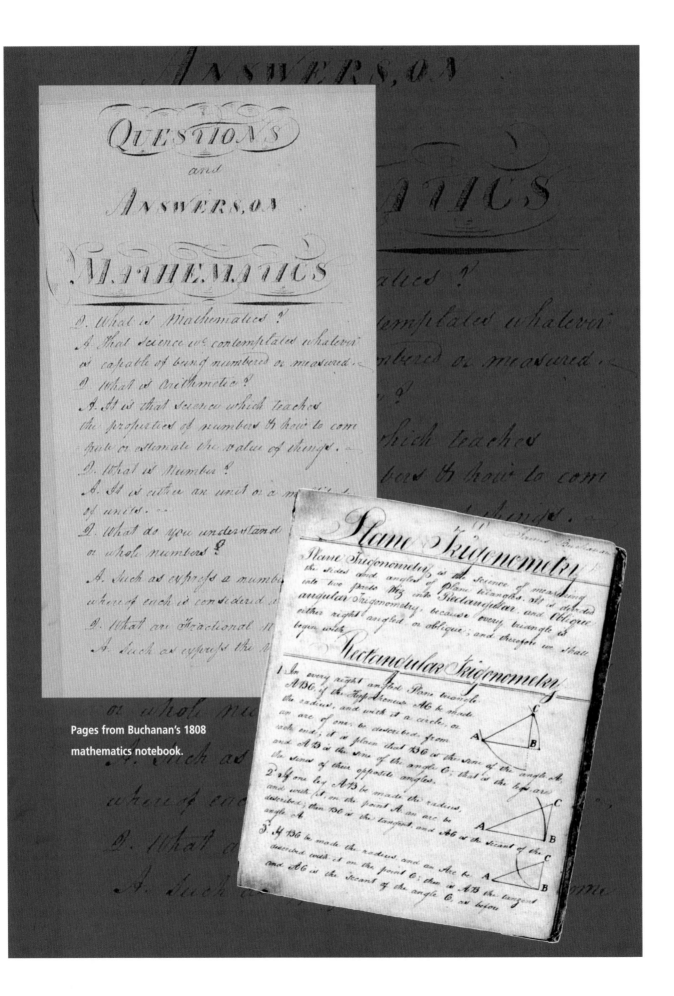

Pages from Buchanan's 1808 mathematics notebook.

Buchanan worked under Tom for four years, and during that time Tom turned a bustling business into a failed enterprise. In June 1787, James Buchanan, a frugal man who was careful to save his money, bought Stony Batter and a hundred surrounding acres for £142 at a tax auction.

Buchanan celebrated his venture into business by marrying his sweetheart, Elizabeth Speer, the daughter of a neighbor of his Uncle Joshua. The Buchanans moved into the log cabin in Cove Gap. Their first child, Mary, died shortly after her birth in 1789. Two years later, son James was born. He was the first of ten more children who would be born into the Buchanan family, although another girl and boy would also die in childhood. Nevertheless, the Buchanans were a robust family and they made father James proud. And there was no question that James was proudest of his oldest son and namesake.

Young James and the other Buchanan children received their early schooling from their mother. Elizabeth Buchanan was well-read; her favorite writers were the poets John Milton, Alexander Pope, and William Cowper, whose works she recited to her children. James was a good listener who absorbed his mother's lessons.

From the words of Milton, Buchanan undoubtedly absorbed some ideas regarding the eternal battle of good against evil, as well as the belief that good will come out of evil. From Cowper, James learned to love the rural life; after retiring from the presidency, Buchanan spent his last years on his rural Pennsylvania estate known as Wheatland and rarely set foot in a big city again. And from Pope, James's natural wit perhaps developed into sarcasm under the influence of Pope's acid invectives, which Buchanan would find useful in debating at Dickinson. It was a talent that would get him in trouble with the faculty but would serve him well as a lawyer and, later, as a lawmaker.

Elizabeth Buchanan also read the Bible to her children and told them stories about George Washington, whom the Buchanans idolized. James and Elizabeth named their youngest son after Washington and may even have met him when the president stayed briefly at Uncle Joshua's tavern in late 1794.

Another early and important teacher was his father. Helping around the Stony Batter trading post, James observed his father's attention to bookkeeping and his fondness for working with numbers. It was the elder Buchanan's belief that John Tom's failure could be attributed to the man's abysmal abilities when it came to calculating numbers. In his later years, son James would be an ardent bookkeeper himself. Even as an occupant of the White House, Buchanan kept scrupulous records of how much he spent and how much he was owed, down to the penny.

With his family growing and business at the trading post turning out to be very prosperous, James Buchanan decided to move out of Cove Gap and into a red-brick home he built on the main street of Mercersburg, a town not far from the Maryland border. Son James was sent to the Old Stone Academy, a one-room schoolhouse in Mercersburg. He was six years old when he enrolled in the school, which was led by a Presbyterian minister, the Reverend James R. Sharon. At the time, there was no law that compelled families to send their children to school.

Even though James was six, his father could have used his help at the trading post or in the fields of the family's adjacent farm. Nevertheless, in County Donegal the elder Buchanan had been sent to school (by his Uncle Samuel, who raised him), so he believed in education and was determined to see his son attend school. For the next ten years, James Buchanan attended school at the Old Stone Academy.

Under the Reverend Sharon and other teachers, James learned Greek, Latin, and mathematics. He was easily the brightest boy in school, although it should be pointed out that the student body at the Old Stone Academy never numbered more than a handful of pupils. Nevertheless, this very sharp young man soon came to the attention of the Reverend John King, the Presbyterian minister in Mercersburg whose authority included overseeing the school.

King was a trustee of Dickinson College. When James turned sixteen, King urged the elder Buchanan to send his boy to Dickinson, about forty miles northeast of Mercersburg. Elizabeth Dickinson had always wanted her eldest son to enter the ministry, but her husband had other ideas. By now, James Buchanan Sr. was the most prosperous businessman and farmer in Mercersburg. He realized that his growing assets would require a keen mind schooled in the complexities of the law to protect his holdings. His son would attend college with the goal of becoming a lawyer so that he might serve his father and look after the Buchanan family interests. In September 1807, James and his father saddled their horses and set out for Carlisle so the boy could enroll in Dickinson College.

The school had been founded in 1783 by Dr. Benjamin Rush, a noted Philadelphia physician and a signer of the Declaration of Independence who believed the young nation needed a college on its western frontier. (The fact that the college was established just a hundred miles west of Philadelphia illustrates where the frontier was in those days.) Rush convinced a number of esteemed citizens to donate to the college and serve on the board of trustees. Among them were James Wilson, soon to be a Supreme Court justice; William Bingham, one of the wealthiest men in Philadelphia; and Ephraim and Robert Blaine, ancestors of future presidential candidate James G. Blaine.

Rush also invited John Dickinson to join the board. A Philadelphian who maintained a farm in Delaware, Dickinson had served in the Continental Congress and later fought in the Continental Army, seeing action at the Battle of Brandywine. His "Letters from a Farmer in Pennsylvania," which were published in a Pennsylvania newspaper in 1767 and 1768, eloquently attacked British taxation policy and urged resistance to unjust laws. The letters earned Dickinson the reputation as "Penman of the Revolution." When Dickinson agreed to donate five hundred acres in Cumberland County as well as a selection of books for the school library, Rush had little trouble convincing the other trustees to name the school after him.

By the time James Buchanan arrived, the college had hardly grown into the prosperous institution its founders had expected. Funds were always short, and Dr. Rush frequently found himself scrambling for money to keep the college going. Since its founding, the college had used an ancient grammar school building on Liberty

Avenue in Carlisle as its main classroom facility. The old building was finally replaced in 1806 by a newly constructed classroom; nevertheless, the money troubles continued. "Suppose we add $10 a year to our tuition money?" Rush proposed in a letter to college officials in 1807. "Education in the present state of our country on an intensive plan should be considered a luxury; and placed only within the reach of persons in easy circumstances. Unless this be the case the proportion of learning will soon over-balance the proportion of labor in our country. Let a plain education…reading, writing and arithmetic be made as cheap as possible, and even free of expense to those who are unable to pay for it. In a Republic no man should have a vote who is unable to read."

Dr. Davidson was one of three professors at the college when Buchanan arrived to join the junior class. The others were Professor John Hayes, who taught languages, and Professor James McCormick, instructor in mathematics. Of the three, Buchanan admired McCormick the most. McCormick and his wife often provided lodgings to students in their home. Unlike the self-important Davidson, McCormick was patient and eager to enjoy a good laugh with his students. When one of his students tested poorly, McCormick would often become quite upset, believing that he had failed in his duty to educate the youth.

At first, Buchanan studied hard. Required reading at Dickinson included the ancient Roman and Greek literary masters—Homer and Cicero among them.

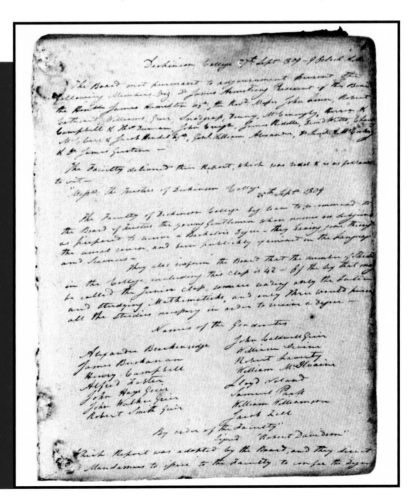

A page from the minutes of the Dickinson College board of trustees meeting, September 27, 1809. During that meeting formal approval was voted for the A.B. degree to be awarded to the fifteen graduates of the class of 1809—whom the board of trustees certified "as prepared to receive their Bachelor's degree, they having gone through the usual courses, and been publicly examined in the Languages and Sciences." Buchanan's name is second down, left column.

This engraving, titled "Dickenson College, 1810" (the college name is misspelled), was based on a sketch done by Buchanan's classmate Alexander Brackenridge.

Cicero's "Catiline Debates" were of particular interest to Buchanan. The orations tell the story of how Cicero used the Roman Senate to unmask and denounce the traitorous Lucius Cataline. "When, O Catiline, do you mean to cease abusing our patience?" Cicero said. "How long is that madness of yours still to mock us? When is there to be an end of that unbridled audacity of yours, swaggering about as it does now?" For someone whose political career would take him first to the legislature of Pennsylvania and then to Congress, Cicero's eloquent arguments to a body of lawmakers surely must have provided Buchanan with inspiration.

Buchanan also pored through the writings of the school's chief benefactor, John Dickinson. There is no question that Dickinson was one of the nation's most devoted patriots. His letters stirred emotions in his fellow colonists and clearly set out a list of grievances that he felt King George was obliged to correct—but he also counseled the colonists against war. In his third letter, Dickinson explained the purpose of his open correspondence. He wrote: "The meaning of the [letters] is to convince the people of these colonies that they are at this moment exposed to the most imminent dangers; and to persuade them immediately, vigorously, and unanimously, to exert themselves, in the most firm, but most peaceful manner, for obtaining relief. The cause of liberty is a cause of too much dignity to be sullied by turbulence and tumult. It ought to be maintained in a manner suitable to her nature. Those who engage in it, should breathe a sedate, yet fervent spirit, animating them to actions of prudence, justice, modesty, bravery, humanity and magnanimity." Nine years later, when Dickinson was serving in the Continental Congress, he participated in the historic debate on independence during the summer of 1776. When the delegates voted for independence, Dickinson refused to sign the declaration. He believed it would lead to war with England, which he opposed.

John Dickinson was a man who stood on his principles, refusing to go along with the majority when he believed it would surely lead to war. More than eight decades later, President James Buchanan would find himself faced with a similar problem. It was Buchanan's steadfast belief that the U.S. Constitution provided no powers to the president to halt the secession of the southern states, which occurred during the last weeks of his administration. Sadly, he stood by that belief as the chasm separating North and South grew ever wider, making bloodshed inevitable.

Buchanan did return to Dickinson for his senior year. After receiving the letter of expulsion from Dr. Davidson, Buchanan approached the Reverend King and asked him to intercede. By then, Buchanan's hometown minister had become president of the Dickinson trustees. "He gave me a gentle lecture," Buchanan recalled. "He then proposed to me that if I would pledge my honor to him to behave better at college than I had done, he felt such confidence in me that he would pledge himself to Dr. Davidson on my behalf, and he did not doubt that I would be permitted to return."

Once back at Dickinson, Buchanan kept his word. He stayed out of Carlisle taverns, spent his nights on his school work, and reined in his sarcastic mouth when called on in class. He joined one of the school's two literary groups, the Union Philosophical Society, and led the organization's lively debates—often practicing his speeches while strolling through town. When the school year ended, the Union Philosophical endorsed Buchanan for senior class valedictorian. The faculty, still smarting over Buchanan's conduct the previous year, selected the choice of the school's other literary group, the Belles Lettres Society.

Buchanan was outraged. So were most of his fellow students, who believed him to be the far superior student. There was talk of a student rebellion—nobody would accept valedictory honors. Finally, the faculty reached a compromise: Buchanan would be permitted to deliver an address at the graduation, but not as valedictorian. Grudgingly, Buchanan agreed. On September 19, 1809, the nation's future president accepted his diploma from Dickinson College.

The graduation incident would forever weigh heavily on Buchanan. Years later, he wrote: "The other members of the society belonging to the senior class would have united with me in refusing to speak at the approaching commencement, but I was unwilling to place them in this situation on my account, and more especially as several of them were designed for the ministry. I held out myself for some time, but at last yielded on receiving a kind communication from the professors. I left college, however, feeling but little attachment towards the Alma Mater."

—Hal Marcovitz